OCCULT
INVESTIGATOR

Real Cases from the Files
of X-Investigations

Bob Johnson

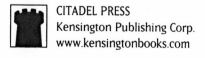

CITADEL PRESS
Kensington Publishing Corp.
www.kensingtonbooks.com

CITADEL PRESS books are published by

Kensington Publishing Corp.
850 Third Avenue
New York, NY 10022

All Kensington titles, imprints, and distributed lines are available at special quantity discounts for bulk purchases for sales promotions, premiums, fund raising, educational, or institutional use. Special book excerpts or customized printings can also be created to fit specific needs. For details, write or phone the office of the Kensington special sales manager: Kensington Publishing Corp., 850 Third Avenue, New York, NY 10022, attn: Special Sales Department; phone 1-800-221-2647.

CITADEL PRESS and the Citadel logo are Reg. U.S. Pat. and TM Off.

First printing: September 2004

10 9 8 7 6 5 4 3 2 1

Printed in the United States of America

Library of Congress Control Number: 2004106004

ISBN 0-8065-2606-8

For Darlene

I love her so much it's scary.

Contents

Acknowledgments

Many thanks to Bruce Bender of Kensington Publishing Corp. and Citadel Books in New York City for giving me yet another opportunity to write about what others either don't believe or are too frightened to admit.

I would also like to thank my editor, Margaret Wolf, for her patience, guidance, and above all her understanding of *why* we do what we do!

Introduction

Van Helsing, Blade, and Buffy battled vampires; Derek Rayne, the mysterious leader of the TV series *Poltergeist: The Legacy*, fought fallen angels; and Father Karras exorcised the Devil himself. So, I suppose it was life imitating art when I approached a licensed New York detective agency to create a special division to investigate occult and paranormal cases. I felt it was time for a hard-nosed approach to aiding the victims of paranormal bad guys. After all, I argued, the world is enamored with the strange and the bizarre, and more important many are literally "haunted" by curses and the unseen. Shouldn't there be an organization like the one represented on *The X-Files*, where people could turn for help with problems others might think are bizarre? On a general level, society just can't be amazed or frightened enough by the world of the occult. Some of pop culture's most successful books focus on the afterlife and how we can communicate with the dead. There's a never-ending fascination with ghosts, haunted houses, witches, devil worship, voodoo, and every manner of monster. So, shouldn't there be a real-life agency dedicated to exploring, investigating, and if need be kicking the ass of a few malevolent demons?

But paranormal investigators, channelers, mediums, would-be "ghost busters," and even professional exorcists, are a dime a dozen, filling the pages of every New Age journal and Web site known. They all claim that they can solve any occult problem that comes along. And many are well versed in the occult world—scholars in their own right who are experts in every field of the dark arts. Many "ghost hunters" are enamored with technical gadgets and spy equipment and are happy to record every bump in the night. But the legion of authors, societies, organizations, and so on lack one important attribute: real-world investigative smarts. Metropolitan police departments always have their token "occult expert," but he or she is usually concerned with murders and heinous acts that the cops can't pin on anyone or anything tangible. And religious organizations will only deal with the Devil— and then only after thousands of hours of testimony and, dare I say it, proper tithing? There are no civil service manuals or tests that one takes to become an investigator, despite the myriad of "paranormal investigation" study courses, societies, schools, and organizations. Even the few universities that actually have programs like Duke University's Rhine Research Center, are much more concerned with true scientific PSI research and collecting tons of data than exposing spooks, demons, or curses.

So, I concluded that people who really needed help— normal people—would only turn to an organization dedicated to investigating strange events—if it could first prove there wasn't any earthly fraud or bilking going on *before* it went after any "other worldly" troublemakers. The new breed of investigative organization needed to have bonafide occult credentials *and* a network in place to first cut through and uncover any dubious obstacles so it could then concentrate on what truly could not be explained.

But enticing a professional firm that's used to uncovering corporate espionage, protecting celebrities, and following would-be criminals to take on a paranormal and occult investigator to bust spooks wasn't easy. Fortunately, I had a substantial background and had studied the occult (I also wrote a book on using magick in the workplace called *Corporate Magick*) and I could tell some pretty scary stories, enough to convince the owner of a prominent New York detective agency to at least open the door to the possibility of taking on an *X-Files*-type crew.

The first question I'm asked is usually accompanied by a smirk and cocked eyebrow, "So . . . how did you become a *ghost buster* in the first place?" And when I met with Vincent, the owner of Intercontinental Investigations in New York, it was no different. So, I had to be honest and say that I never set out to become a ghost buster in the literal sense of the word, even though I admit the movie of that name was rather cool for its time. I told him about my idea to create a new kind of paranormal investigative agency—one that could bust ghosts and frauds all at once. Vincent was intrigued and asked me to explain my background.

The short story was that my interest in all things occult started at a very early age when the mundane aspects of life gave way to the fantastic worlds of witches, ghosts, and demons. When I first discovered that there was another world— a dark side—that secretly coexisted with our everyday grind, I began to make it my business to explore that more mysterious and bizarre plane where people see floating images at their bedposts at night, hear moans and screams coming from abandoned rooms, and are plagued by magical "curses." It excited me to think that the stuff of horror movies could be true. I fantasized that maybe there really were witches casting spells on people and flying on their brooms at night while I lay asleep in bed. Maybe vampires really did have those awesome powers to fly like bats and dematerialize into fog. If these pilgrims of the night actually existed, I wanted to find them, to meet them, and most of all to learn how they made their magic.

It was a hobby at first, reading the school library books on ghosts, psychics, mediums, and strange creatures. But my appetite for the occult grew with an epiphany. I came across the book *Ghosts I've Met,* by preeminent ghost hunter, lecturer, and occult expert Dr. Hans Holzer (who coincidentally later became my friend, advisor, and professor at the New York Committee for the Investigation of Paranormal Occurrences). Holzer's book was not the run-of-the-mill ghost book—he named names, as they say. His eyewitness accounts of paranormal events were so vividly described that by today's standards the book would have immediately been made into a reality TV series. Holzer didn't just write about ghosts and the occult, he lived in that world. That first book of his and subsequent titles took me by the hand and said, "See, there really are ghosts and witches and this is who they are and where they live." Another milestone was when I interviewed the late Dr. Raymond McNally for my college newspaper. McNally is the author of *In Search of Dracula*—the first real investigative work on the Dracula myth that opened the doors to Transylvania as more than a mythical place of monsters. The dedicated author was also a scholarly and levelheaded person who took the dark side seriously. Eureka! I finally had hard facts that can *prove* the unreal is real. That's all I needed. I was hooked on scary stuff, and even if I didn't believe what I couldn't see, the yearning to uncover the mysterious became my quest.

My obsession lasted for years, and despite my enthusiasm I always looked at every description of a paranormal event with a skeptical eye, more so that I wouldn't be disappointed than as a nonbeliever. But I hadn't found any hard evidence to support a bona fide paranormal event. Sure, I visited a number of haunted houses and attended a myriad of occult ceremonies and rituals, but I had never been blown away by what I witnessed. No ethereal wisps flew around the room, no demons spun their heads off and shot green vomit at me, and I never, ever saw a ghost. That was until I went to work as a reporter for an occult news magazine in the early 1970's called *Beyond Reality*. After a few months writing about Bigfoot, UFOs, and vampire graves, my editor assigned me to stay overnight at the infamous Amityville Horror house on Long Island. The results are stuff for another book, but the experience made me a believer that—regardless of how they are described—there *are* other planes of existence that we have only the vaguest clues about.

After a few hours of chatting and recounting my own brand of ghost story (and bringing in Silvana, my "Emma Peel-like" psychic Czech colleague, dressed in her catwoman leather outfit), Vincent and I decided to create a specialized arm of his detective agency dedicated to cases involving the occult and paranormal. I christened the groundbreaking agency X-Investigations—the world's only paranormal agency affiliated with a licensed detective agency that had the resources to solve cases in both this world and the next!

The stories that follow are based on real investigations straight from X-Investigations' private files that have been chosen to allow you to draw your own conclusions as to whether the events were truly paranormal. Some have photographic evidence to help you decide. Others will baffle you. The names of the clients have been changed to protect people who are concerned that they would be labeled "crackpots" or witches if their peers and neighbors discovered their dilemmas. Some were frightened about retribution from the occult world.

Sit back and become an armchair detective with a Sam Spade of the supernatural. And by the way . . . *now*, who ya gonna call?—www.x-investigations.com!

OCCULT
INVESTIGATOR

I.

The Curse of the Velvet Room Café

It haunted her like she had committed a murder. Each time Mary Montrose entered the Velvet Room Café on the Upper East Side of Manhattan, a sense of fearful dread overcame her. She felt guilty, evil, ugly, and even sinful. She felt as if she had done something terribly wrong and she would somehow have to pay a horrible price. But what troubled her most was not the feeling of darkness, but the confusion in her mind as to why she should feel these things. She was not an evil person. She had done nothing to harm anyone in her life that would warrant these awful, malignant impressions.

And what was even more disturbing was that this feeling attacked her only when she visited the quaint Madison Avenue café. The shop pleased her so much, as it was decorated in the rich, ornate, and lush Victorian period style. She loved the place. She loved the velvety soft sofas and how the cascading drapery framed the large front window. When she looked out of the window onto Second Avenue, through the purple and red drapery, she imagined herself a Victorian lady waiting for her gentleman's carriage. Her heart beat rapidly and her face flushed during her café daydreams. But the glow was quickly overcome by that gnawing, ominous sense of depression that leaked into her mind and body, almost causing her to bolt from the café in a panic.

Mary simply couldn't understand how a café, a storefront, could evoke such a terrible feeling within her. The first time she noticed it was in the winter of 1995—just after Christmas. She remembered it vividly because the New York holiday lull between Christmas Day and New Year's Day stood out in her mind. She recalled how she desperately tried to hang on to her usual festive and secure feeling between the two occasions, but then remembered how it was suddenly interrupted by the Velvet Room Café's sullen shadow.

It began after a full morning's shopping along Madison Avenue at her favorite boutiques, when Mary decided she needed a coffee break to recharge her energy for the remainder of the day. Although she vaguely remembered a small café that she promised herself she would one day visit, she couldn't put her finger on its name or where it was located. Mary knew it appealed to her because of its décor and ambience and that it seemed to "pop up" whenever she was shopping nearby, but she had no real sense of where the little shop actually was. She was determined to find the haven so she could rest her tired feet and also satisfy her curiosity about the café. Walking aimlessly and peering down side streets looking for the shop, she was just about to give up and enter a Starbucks when a screeching taxicab jumped the curb of 56th Street, taking out a mailbox, three street signs, and nearly crushing her into a plate-glass window. She was knocked off of her feet but she fortunately managed to avoid being seriously hurt.

Once Mary caught her breath and shook the cobwebs from her head, she assured the group of people who circled around her that she was indeed not hurt. She then walked a few steps, looked up, and was amazed to see that she was directly in front of the storefront she was looking for. The Velvet Room Café's ornamental sign seemed to stare at her like a welcoming beacon and she instinctively entered the store, unaware that her respite was to be the beginning of a harrowing journey into the supernatural that carried with it a malignant ancient curse, strange apparitions, and a greedy, deranged blood relation who would affect her life for years to come.

Ghost Hunters

When I pitched the idea for the creation of a special unit of Intercontinental Investigations, a prominent New York City detective agency, that would seriously investigate paranormal and occult cases, I expected to get a lukewarm response and possibly some feigned interest from my friend who owned the agency, mostly out of respect and a mutual understanding of my interest in "things peculiar." But when he responded with sincere interest and began to recount stories of his Italian grandmother (thought to be a *strega*, an Italian witch), who regularly communicated with the dead, threw curses, and was responsible for at least a few "mysterious" deaths in their small Italian village, I knew I had a shot at developing what was to be X-Investigations, the first paranormal and occult investigative arm of a licensed detective agency.

My background investigating the occult and the paranormal to this point was not a professional one. Although I had consulted numerous times with the preeminent ghost hunter and author Dr. Hans Holzer, and earned a certificate from his New York Committee for the Investigation of Paranormal Occurrences, my investigations had been mostly of an academic nature, albeit fulfilling in their own right. Most of my experiences centered on the "possibilities" of paranormal and occult workings, more than actual sightings or firsthand encounters with the unexplained. That was until I attended a ghost hunting excursion with the International Ghost Hunters Society in Salem, Massachusetts, which opened up a fascinating and sometimes frightening world of the unexplained and often disturbing glimpses of the "other side."

Toward the end of the first day's field work exercise, which included a walk through a local cemetery and instructions that a ghost hunter must "respect the dead" by asking their permission to photograph their resting places, our group headed for a building on Essex Street in the center of the town's commercial pedestrian mall that once was a colonial library building, now converted into a local retail establishment. The wood frame store was vacant for the most part—quite large and creepy by most standards—with huge open rooms filled with covered furniture accentuated by the store's high ceilings and a central staircase that wound around to a landing with doors to a number of rooms on the second level. The building gave our group needed shelter from the cold Salem October night, but curiously did not feel secure. Although the temperature was warmer inside than outdoors, it was still surprisingly damp and somehow uninviting. The yellow cloud-covered Moon shone intermittently through the windows on the upper floors of the building and at first was the only light we saw as we entered. Everyone in our group briskly rubbed warmth into their hands and commented that it was good to be out of the cold, but as we ventured further into the darkness, waiting for the lights to be switched on, we became silent—as if we were waiting for someone to say, "It's all right. The lights will be on in a minute and we'll all feel safe and warm." But no one spoke, and after about five minutes of standing in the glistening moonlit ground floor waiting for the caretaker to find the fuse box, some of us became "antsy," demanding some light. I was not the only one who said the place felt strange and foreboding . . . almost evil.

Our instruction from Dave, the stout, bearded fellow in charge of the ghost hunting organization, was to scout around the building, using our Gauss meters (devices that measure electromagnetic variance, a standard ghost hunting apparatus) and cameras in order to capture any paranormal activity. Our group broke up into small parties with the bravest of us venturing into the back rooms and deserted hallways, looking for spirits or whatever unworldly manifestation might occur. I took it on myself to head to the farthest room in the back of the building with one of my fellow ghost hunters, Betsy, a middle-aged grammar school teacher from Lubbock, Texas, who was armed with a state-of-the-art digital camera. I wondered if Betsy knew what she was doing with such a high-tech camera. Her large, ill-fitting black eyeglasses and frumpy manner didn't exactly speak of technical proficiency, but I admired her for her courage nonetheless.

We both walked gingerly into the center of the room, turning our heads from side to side as if we were cartoon characters in a *Scooby Doo* episode waiting for the typical malevolent force to strike out. But this was no cartoon. Immediately after entering the room, we were both overcome by a feeling of being watched—the kind of feeling that prompts people to jerk their necks around to see who's there. We also felt a strange presence emanating from a darkened portion of the room directly beneath a window that stretched from the floor to almost ten feet in height. I couldn't see anyone or anything, but I knew instinctively that there was something crouching in the dark. I felt its coldness cutting a path in the air right toward my face. An instant later, Betsy and I both turned around to see if there was someone looking over our shoulders. Of course, no one was present, causing us to look each other in the eyes and exchange a nonverbal agreement to just keep walking. Any other acknowledgment of this strange feeling would only make it all the more real.

Despite our fear, a distinct feeling of dread, and a strong urge to run out of that damp room, we headed toward the area in question to investigate why it reeked so strongly of something unknown. After all, that's why we were on this trip, to discover a ghost or some other paranormal event, so now was not the time to run screaming.

I clicked on my handheld plastic Gauss meter and watched the black needle hover at the green-colored low end of its Miligauss (mG) range of 0 to 2, which usually indicates nearly virtually no electromagnetic activity. Betsy sighed a breath of relief and began to snap some digital photos of the area. But her relief soon ended when I placed the Gauss meter at the bottom of the window—the area where we sensed the crouching presence—and the needle literally jumped through the safe green and yellow areas of its dial from 0 to 2 mG to the meter's red zone of 7 to 20 mG, whirring violently in my hand. I yelled to Betsy that she had to look at what was going on with my meter. But instead of running to see for herself, the photographer in Betsy instinctively took over and she began snapping photos of me holding the Gauss meter at the bottom of the window. I managed not to move from my position for a good five minutes so Betsy could click away, all the while transfixed by the windshield wiper motion of the meter's needle snapping back and forth. Something was present in this spot, I was certain of that much, and I was grateful that Betsy had the presence of mind to take pictures while I was frantically yelling for my colleagues to watch this phenomenon. Needless to say, I was spooked, and I'm the first to admit that a big reason why I stayed glued to the spot was that I was literally paralyzed by fear.

Thanks to the instantaneous feedback from the digital camera, we would be able to see right away just what, if anything, would show up in the photos Betsy snapped. Two of the most common manifestations of spirits caught on camera, according to Dave, are white wisp apparitions that appear like smoke or round floating objects called "orbs" that can be spotted almost anywhere in the picture, but usually not in front of or on top of a person.

I watched closely as Betsy thumbed the top of her camera, searching through the shots, not truly convinced that we were going to see anything out of the ordinary. But then Betsy curiously stopped fidgeting with the buttons on the camera. Her gaze became fixed and her face literally blanched. She first whispered some inaudible expletive to herself, and then suddenly blurted out, "You are not going to fucking believe this. Look at this shot!"

She handed the camera over to me and as I brought the small rectangular image close enough to see what was there, I became speechless. It was a photo of me holding the Gauss meter at the bottom of the window. But what caused us both to look at the photo with dropped jaws was the image of a large white orb that sat hovering precisely at the top of the meter as though it had landed on my electronic instrument! More of Betsy's shots showed the orb moving first toward the meter and then upward toward the top of the window. Goosebumps, hair standing on the back of the neck, and spine tingling chills; none of these words can accurately describe our sensations when we saw the photos. And what was even more upsetting was that we were now feeling that presence again, along with the coldness. We sensed a force very close by and we had two technical devices confirming as much as possible that we were witnessing a manifestation of something unexplainable in "normal" terms. There was no electrical current near the Gauss meter, nor any electrical wiring in the walls that would have sent the mechanism into its wild behavior. There was no possibility of "spots" on the film in a digital camera because there is no film. And Betsy was certain that her camera lens had been cleaned and air dusted right before she left her hotel room. There was only one logical conclusion: *We had felt and seen something paranormal and possibly supernatural. We had captured a ghost!*

The Birth of X-Investigations

My conversation about creating a special unit to concentrate on the paranormal and occult in Vincent's detective agency, to this point, was mainly a friendly discussion and a fact-finding mission on his part to determine if there really was anything to my idea. We kicked around the possibilities, often returning to the problem of whether people would think they (Vincent and his business) were a bit loony, but there was no solid commitment much less an invitation fron Vincent to provide some proof that this kind of business could succeed.

But all that changed after my Salem excursion. I was now confident that when I returned to New York from my ghost hunting adventure with bonafide digital evidence of a real ghost sighting, Vincent would be a lot more receptive and a lot less skeptical. What I didn't bargain for was that when I got back to my Manhattan apartment I would find a message on my telephone answering machine from a woman at Vincent's office who identified herself only as Silvana, saying that she was working with Vincent on a "special" case that involved things she described as "out of the ordinary." Of course, I was pleasantly surprised and intrigued both with the nature of the message and with Silvana's interesting east European accent that I couldn't directly place. I'm usually pretty adept at discerning peoples' origins from their accents, but because the message contained a sense of urgency tinged with underlying concern or worry, Silvana's linguistic origin was a tough call.

Silvana's message had been left on the same day of my haunted library excursion in Salem and she said that Vincent thought this case was especially suited for the two of us. Even though we had never worked together, Silvana said that I shouldn't be concerned about how she knew Vincent, or me for that matter, or what the case entailed, but that I should call and meet with her as soon as possible. She added that she wasn't worried about the lack of any formal framework within Vincent's organization for paranormal investigations. She said,

"This is the kind of investigation most people would think is bizarre and possibly crazy. But . . . you now know, as do I, that there are many things that cannot be explained, and there are but a few of us who are more than just curious . . . we are destined to uncover the unexplained."

At first, I thought Vincent was playing one of his infamous practical jokes, goading me into thinking that he had come around to forming the special unit, so I'd rush into his office, arms flailing and spouting a hundred ideas. He'd then burst out with the bogus "Silvana" laughing hysterically next to him. But the next message on my machine confirmed what Silvana had said. It was Vincent's secretary, Barbara, who was always as serious as death and never known to goof around. Barbara said Vincent was out of town but that I should call Silvana immediately. "It is very important."

Not knowing who Silvana was, or if she even existed, and still not convinced that this wasn't a trick of some kind, I instead waited until Vincent returned to town in the next few days. I didn't want some nutty joke overshadowing the real proof I just uncovered and ruining the possibility of realizing X-Investigations.

I visited the offices of Intercontinental Investigations one rainy Tuesday morning with Betsy's borrowed digital camera in hand. I was adamant about convincing Vincent about my paranormal experience, so I knew I had to put the evidence right on his desk so he could see it with his own eyes. He greeted me as cordially as usual, but before I could say a word, he asked if I had contacted Silvana. When I told him that I hadn't, he became curiously agitated and said that Silvana had just the case I was looking for to start X-Investigations. Before he could pick up the phone to call her, I stuck the camera under his nose with the glowing photo and said, "Vincent, I'm glad you said that. Now look at these photos. Tell me what you see."

"I see you holding some gadget in an old house with a blob of light reflecting on the picture." I told him that this was no blob of light but an actual ghostly orb captured digitally. "C'mon, this is a picture of a ghost? It's dust on the lens," Vincent said. It took me the better part of an hour of raised eyebrows and Vincent snickering to convince him that orbs are one of the most common paranormal phenomena photographed, and I described in detail the coldness, the malevolent feelings, and the lurking presence in the dark that both Betsy and I felt. It took some doing, but Vincent knew that if I was this passionate about something he'd better listen. After an intense accounting of what took place at the Salem library, Vincent became mesmerized and by the end of my tale he was hanging on every word. When I showed him the remainder of the orb photos, he simply said, "I've got chills running up and down my spine. But I need more proof."

The detective agency often used forensic specialists to investigate and analyze the most obscure evidence and clues imaginable, and although I suspected that most of Vincent's experts never did much ghost hunting, I suggested to him that he have the camera analyzed by one of his associates to validate the legitimacy of the photo and determine whether there was any "normal" interference that may have caused the appearance of the orb. If there were dust or reflections on the lens, these could be detected by his modern-day supersleuths. If they didn't find any evidence of this, I was sure that I could convince Vincent that other worlds existed beyond our own, and more important persuade him to back my fledgling idea to help discover why these worlds exist and why they often intrude on this plane of existence we call "reality."

It didn't take long for Felix, Vincent's forensic photography expert, to give us the results in the detective's office a few days later. His report stated that from all of the data supplied to him, the camera, its digital disc, and its optics were working just fine. He also reported that the digital images taken by Betsy that night were not tampered with in any way. There were no scratches on the camera lens, and there was no discernible dirt or dust. Felix added that any reflection that would have appeared on the photo would not have caused such a porous image, but would rather have appeared solid. He told us that a light reflection would have "blurred" deeply and the orb on the photo was nearly transparent. The bottom line was that Felix delivered the honest answers I'd hoped to hear: the photos were legitimate and the orb appearance could not be explained. For all intents and purposes, we had caught a ghost on camera!

Feeling vindicated and confident that I could make a go of X-Investigations, I asked Vincent straight out if we could use his office as headquarters. He still wasn't convinced about the viability of a ghost busting occult investigations division of his company, but he remembered Silvana and her almost frantic plea to him about a woman in dire need of help . . . not normal private detective assistance, but something requiring specialized expertise. He told me that I should first speak with Silvana to see what her situation involved. If we could fit it all together, Vincent said he'd back our endeavor.

Silvana had given Vincent only a sketchy idea of our would-be maiden case. The most he knew was that it involved a woman on the East Side who had a recurring problem with "unknown forces" and that she was at her wits' end. "There was something about her freaking out at a café and the owner was threatening to sue her if she didn't stop harassing his café about a curse or some nonsense," Vincent told me. I knew that there was something Vincent was reluctant to tell me . . . that was his style, tease a case so the investigator got interested enough to flesh out the details and eventually got so absorbed in the investigation that it became an obsession. But he didn't have to play games to get me involved with this case. I figured that any case that would launch X-Investigations was worth pursuing. I wasted no time and called Silvana that evening at her home. What she told me not only piqued my curiosity, but it allowed me a *peek* at a world only a few dare to visit.

She answered the phone with a distinct Czech accent, "Ahhlow." I began to introduce myself by saying "I am . . ." but she cut me off in midsentence and said, "I know who you are, Mr. Johnson. You have waited too long to contact me. We must act quickly, for there is a woman's life at stake." Before I could ask her how she knew it was me, she said that she was a clairvoyant and medium with psychic abilities, and if I needed proof she said I was to meet with her that very evening.

"If you're psychic," I said, "then you should know where I'm thinking about meeting right now." I waited for an answer but the phone line was dead. "Weird," I thought. But then my apartment buzzer rang and the doorman said I had a message left downstairs that said the meeting that evening concerning the woman in need was to be at my favorite coffee house, Manzo's, in Little Italy. I asked the doorman who left the message and he said that all he could remember was that she was a "tall babe with a great body and an accent." He couldn't remember her name, but he said she was worth going to the meeting for, no matter where it was, even if it was pouring an icy November rain outdoors.

As I got out of the cab on Kenmare Street in front of Manzo's to meet the mysterious Silvana, I gathered my umbrella and immediately had a sensation that I was about to see an old friend, not a new acquaintance. Maybe it was wishful thinking or a carry-over sense of familiarity from our phone conversation, but when I entered the café and saw Silvana sipping an espresso and dressed in a black turtleneck sweater, black leather skirt, and deep violet tights with *Sex in the City* designer pointed half-boots, I felt as though I was about to reconnect with an old relative or an old flame. It didn't hurt that she was stunningly beautiful . . . tall, slender with dark eyes and dark hair. She was a bit of a "beatnik," combined with some of *The Avengers'* Emma Peel TV character thrown in. But my first impression of her as a sophisticated European was mixed with a feeling that Silvana harbored some dark secrets. I felt that she was troubled, not by mundane problems, but by something that could be described as inky, murky, almost ancient. Silvana stood tall and straight when she saw me enter. She greeted me with a firm handshake and warm but questioning eyes. In her Czech accent, she said it was a pleasure to meet me, and then she got right down to business. She told me of a woman who was cursed . . . not by a person, but by a store, a café right here in Manhattan. Mary Montrose had contacted her some weeks before, after learning of Silvana's psychic abilities. With no one else to turn to, Mary had sought Silvana's help in ridding herself of the awful occurrences that haunted her daily life.

They were strange indeed, the fits of hysteria, the cold winds in her room, the smell of vomit in her kitchen, and the constant disappearance of her money. Mary's life was becoming a nightmare. And as Silvana recounted Mary's story to me for the better part of two hours, I finally realized what was behind Silvana's questioning eyes, She could *feel* the other side and the entities that inhabited it, but she could do nothing about it. She was virtually paralyzed by her own perceptive powers. Silvana was a paranormal conduit who needed help from someone who could stay grounded on this plane. That's where I came in.

The next morning in Vincent's midtown offices over deli coffee and bagels, I explained to Silvana my idea to start X-Investigations and how her calling me and seeking help with Mary Montrose was serendipitous, to say the least. She wasn't very concerned with the business of solving occult cases. Silvana's more burning issue was to fulfill her "calling," but she agreed that having a framework for this kind of assistance was a good idea. When I asked her if she was interested in becoming my partner and that she would have to undergo some paranormal abilities testing, she simply smiled at me and told me the exact date that my mother passed away, that my father was still alive, and what hospital I was born in in Brooklyn. I told her that that was pretty good party-game psychicism, but any good detective could have simply looked up those records on the Internet. But when she told me that my old cat Szandor liked to eat lasagna, I was stunned. "Now how did you know *that*?" I asked. She smiled and said, "Vincent told me."

I gave Silvana the benefit of the doubt and we became paranormal partners on the spot.

We began mapping out X-Investigations as a business with a plan to call Mary Montrose that afternoon and get that case under way. We didn't know what our fees would be or what equipment and/or other professionals we would need to conduct our investigations, but we knew we had an enigma on our hands. Silvana did know, however, that Mary appeared to be well off financially and she even mentioned that money was no object—Silvana pointed out that Mary wore an expensive initial "M" diamond brooch. "Robert [she refused to call me "Bob"], it *moost* have cost two or three *hundert towsand* Amerikan dollars," Silvana said. At the very least, we could tell Vincent that we were not working for free.

I asked Silvana to tell me in detail about Mary's bizarre dilemma, and the more she relayed, the more I felt this would be more than just our first case—it would be an adventure into the unknown. I can't explain why, I just *knew* we were embarking on a fantastic experience—one that would haunt us for days to come.

Mary Montrose answered her telephone in a strained tone. "Hello, Miss Montrose, this is Bob Johnson, I am an associate of Silvana's."

At that point, Mary interrupted me and said that she was terribly troubled. "Yes, yes, I know who you are. Can you help me? Do you know what I've been going through these past few weeks?" She was frantically rambling so I had to stop her by asking for her address and when we could visit her. I asked if we could perhaps meet at the Velvet Room Café, the origin of her troubles. She snapped back that that was the last place she wanted to be right now. "The last time I was in the café I was taken away in an ambulance and spent two days in the psychiatric ward at St. Vincent's hospital. Please, please come to my home."

Silvana and I arrived at Mary's apartment around 7:00 that evening. The weather had gotten progressively worse, now mixing sleet and snowflakes with the icy rain, so we were happy to enter the warm lobby of Mary's luxury apartment building. The traditionally cozy Mediterranean décor, the fire in the lobby fireplace, and the hospitable concierge gave us a sense of security on entering. But the glow soon vanished when we heard Mary's unsettling ghost story.

The well-dressed middle-aged woman served us tea and specialty chocolate cookies that I recognized were from an expensive Upper East Side food boutique. All indications were that Mary was a product of fine upbringing and was no stranger to the better things in life. Despite the graciousness of the moment, Mary sighed deeply and began telling us how she was literally thrown into the Velvet Room Café by virtue of an errant taxicab that jumped the curb, nearly killing her. "It was the strangest thing. I was shopping and a bit tired so I thought I would have some coffee at a small, lovely café I had spotted many times before but never had the time to visit. I really could not remember where it was located, but I recalled it was lavishly decorated in Victorian fashion, so I just started to wander along Madison Avenue. Suddenly, I heard screeching and the next thing I knew I was laying near the café with people rushing around asking me if I was all right and if I needed a doctor. Well, once I gathered my senses I was pleased to discover that I had at *least* reached the destination I sought, so I accepted the shop owner's gracious offer of tea and scones gratis for my trouble," Mary recounted.

She then explained how she admired the Velvet Room Cafe's décor—the beautiful and lush drapery, the ornate wallpaper, and the gilded furniture. As she sipped her tea, Mary was pleased with the sense of warmth she got from the café and decided she would visit as often as she could. Then the unexplained began to happen. As Mary was nibbling on her blueberry scone, she felt a tightening in her throat. At first, she thought that maybe she was allergic to some ingredient in the pastry, but she had eaten blueberry scones many times before. They were her favorite. She was puzzled by what was causing this odd sensation. Then things got worse. The strangling feeling increased, and all at once the walls of the room seemed to be closing in on her. Was this odd feeling a delayed reaction to the near-accident, she wondered? She couldn't think straight. She told Silvana and me that it hadn't felt like an ordinary illness, but rather that something had crept into her throat and was choking her from the *inside*. The walls of the café moved toward Mary in an ominous, threatening manner so powerfully that it caused her to drop the scone and shriek, freezing the patrons and café workers in their very footsteps.

She could barely speak as she told us of her horrifying experience. But I insisted that she continue, telling us in as much detail as possible so we could get a handle on what we were dealing with. I instructed Silvana to begin tape recording when we entered the apartment, so everything Mary said was documented. "Of course, Mary, this could have been an aftershock, so to speak, from your trauma that day, as you already mentioned," I said. But Mary told us that she had a medical checkup the very next day that suggested nothing abnormal. More important, the café incident was just the first in a series of harrowing experiences that had followed her home.

"They are *not* all physical manifestations of that trauma. Things are happening in this apartment that have nothing to do with me physically. I feel as though I am being watched, taunted, and punished for something. I am being haunted," she said, choking back tears.

With that remark, X-Investigations experienced its first paranormal anomaly! It was at that point we heard a rapid tapping sound. At first, we thought the sound came from frozen rain pellets beating against Mary's living room window, but as she turned her head into the bedroom, we realized the sound was coming from within the room. "There, see, it's happening," she said in a much more agitated voice. "There's that infernal rapping on the painting above my bed. It happens almost every evening. It's driving me mad."

I asked if Silvana and I could enter the room and Mary told us to go right ahead, but to be very careful. "Sometimes things fly across the room," she warned. When we entered through the double doors, we first noticed the coldness of the room and thought that the heat was turned off. The sensation reminded me of my Salem ghost experience. I could literally see Silvana's breath mist in the dim light. Yes, it was cold in New York, but luxury digs are kept warm for sure. And the living area was very comfortable. Something out of the ordinary was happening in Mary's bedroom. But before we could identify what caused the tapping sounds in the room, we heard a loud shout from the living room where we had left Mary sitting. A scream of *"Get the fuck out, you fucking whoremasters,"* echoed throughout the apartment, apparently coming from where Mary was seated.

We rushed into the living room and saw her slumped in her chair, mouth agape, and staring into space. We were sure it was her making the sounds because we were in the room in an instant and there was no way anyone else could have entered. Her flesh was cold to the touch and a thin stream of

saliva slid down her chin. We called her name, but she continued to stare, so we shook her shoulders until we were able
to rouse some consciousness in her. The living room was now
as cold as the bedroom and the steam from all of our breathing was evident in the air. The parlor was filled with panic
and an eerie sensation that both Silvana and I later agreed
was like nothing we had ever before experienced. It was dreadful and lonely. It was like the feeling you get if you're left
alone at a wake, the only person in the room with the body,
Silvana said.

"Mary, Mary what's wrong . . . what happened?" I asked
her as Silvana rubbed Mary's hands and wrists to help her to
revive. Mary could barely speak, but she told us that something had taken control of her and she could not be responsible for her actions. After a few minutes, she told us that since
that day in the café, nothing had been the same. She felt as
though she was cursed by a malevolent force that somehow
entered her in the Velvet Room Café, in the middle of the
afternoon on an autumn day in Manhattan. Mary recounted
how she went back to the café after the first episode in an
effort to ease her mind and prove to herself that the panic
attack she first experienced there was nothing more than a
physical reaction to the earlier choking trauma. But after only
a few moments at the shop's counter, strange things began
again. This time the brass antique espresso machine behind
the counter erupted, spurting hot coffee in the face of the
waitress, and splashing onto Mary's arm, nearly scalding her.
Mary ran screaming from the café into the street, sobbing hysterically as she hurried home.

"But that's not all, " she continued. "The bad things got
worse. I returned to the café for the third time and sat there

for about ten minutes despite the shopkeeper, Mr. Langley's, apprehension about me possibly causing another scene. My stay was fine for a short while. That was until my order was served. I asked for an orange muffin and hot chocolate with whipped cream, a dish that I have been fond of since I was a child. It always makes me feel secure, conjuring memories of my happy childhood. That was until the waitress placed my order on the table in front of me. I thought I was hallucinating because I saw the muffin jump . . . move a bit. When I lifted it, there were literally hundreds of crawling, black, multilegged silverfish insects stuck to the bottom of the muffin and squirming on the plate. I was transfixed by the horrible sight, not believing my eyes. My first impulse was to call for the waitress and complain, but I couldn't move. I was virtually paralyzed by the sickening creatures darting in and out of the muffin and jumping into my hot chocolate." With that last statement, Mary began to sob uncontrollably. "I need help. Something not of this world is cursing my life. Please, whatever you can do to free me I will appreciate. I've heard of poltergeists and possessions. I know I'm sane in every way, but no one takes me seriously. I turn to you to deal with what I believe is the unseen," Mary said.

On our way back to our respective apartments and crowded into another damp, cold cab, Silvana and I agreed that Mary was as sane as she claimed and was very possibly the victim of a malevolent force. It is common knowledge among those who study human nature as it applies to curses and possessions that if one believes ever so slightly in superstitions of any kind, their susceptibility to superstitious "suggestion" is always present. It was our job to discover whether Mary was somehow contacted by someone, exposed to something that set this "curse" mode in motion in her life, or if in fact was truly cursed. It was X-Investigations' first case, and it was a baffling one. Our first step was to visit the café the next day to witness the origin of Mary Montrose's haunting.

We called Mr. Langley, the owner of the café, the following morning but he said that the only time he had free was near closing, around 11:00 P.M., so if we wanted to meet we'd have to make it late. Silvana and I arrived just as the store clerk was about to lock the front door. Fortunately, we saw Langley and asked the clerk to tell him who we were. He greeted us with some suspicion, not understanding that we weren't detectives looking to nail him on something, but paranormal investigators simply associated with a detective agency. Once we told him that we had been hired by Mary, he nodded and said, "Oh yes, the crazy lady who thinks my café is haunted."

Langley described Mary's experiences almost exactly as Mary did herself, without Mary's description of internal terror. "Something really spooked that woman. We all just thought she was nuts, but I'll admit there were bugs in her food, and that's very odd here because I keep an immaculate kitchen. It never happened before, and it hasn't happened since. And . . . she carried a Bible with her the last time she was here. Guess it didn't help. We thought she was odd but it got us thinking about Jeremy's problem," Langley said. "Jeremy's problem?" I asked. "Yeah, we had a worker here that used to close up the shop. He said he saw strange things going on. You know, he saw shadows, things being moved without his knowledge, wispy smoke coming from the cellar door, crazy shit like that. But it didn't happen all of the time, so we just thought he was loony too," Langley said.

"And, oh yeah, Jeremy said it all started when he found the old docket in the cellar filled with deeds for this place from the turn of the eighteenth century." I was about to ask to see the old papers when Silvana grabbed my wrist tightly and whispered to me that she felt a presence in the room. I could see the sweat bead on her upper lip as she tried to control herself. She was squirming in her chair as Langley went on about the papers, describing the original deeds and the voluminous legal documents. "They might be worth some money, huh?" Langley asked.

Silvana became more agitated. Her eyes were half-closed and her breathing intensified so noticeably that Langley became alarmed. "Hey, what's wrong with her?" he asked.

I told him that she was a clairvoyant and that she was experiencing some kind of paranormal manifestation. "She's being contacted or she's becoming part of your ghost, Mr. Langley," I said. During this disturbing episode, the Velvet Room Café became cold . . . as cold as Mary's bedroom the evening before. Now all of our exhalations were evident as smoky wisps. Langley turned pale as Silvana said to me in between gasps that we must leave the café and that she would explain when we left. At that very moment my cell phone rang. It was Mary, and she was screaming a plea for help. She was crying that her apartment was literally seething with activity. The wall paintings were banging, drawers opening, the toilets were bubbling and backing up water, and she was in fear of her life. I told her that we would be right over and asked her not to call the police. I rushed Silvana out of the café and told Langley we would be back. He stood there in a daze with a baffled and frightened look on his face. We heard him yelling as we left, "Is my café haunted? What the hell . . . ?"

On the ride to Mary's, Silvana told me that there was a force—a disturbed, vengeful presence—that was attempting to settle the score for itself. It was connected with the café and the old papers found in the cellar and Mary was somehow involved. Silvana warned me that the thing was at its final stages on this plane and whatever was to transpire would happen quickly. I had only known Silvana for a few days, but I could see in her eyes that she was dead serious about whatever grasped her in the café. Until this point, she had been witty and often a bit sarcastic. Now, she seemed truly troubled by what we were facing.

We expected to see a trashed apartment when we arrived at Mary's, but we never expected to see Mary herself in such a horrific condition. Her clothes were drenched in sweat, her hair was completely disheveled, and her eyes were teary and bloodshot. The place stank, as though old gym clothes had been left in piles for days gathering mold and mildew. Mary, too, smelled of perspiration and could barely speak when we entered the apartment. She said that this was the worst event yet. After her home had been violently tossed by the bizarre eruptions, the entity appeared. "I saw terrible faces in the mirrors . . . they were sickly pale and looked at me with dreadful eyes. The cold stares were unbearable; I was paralyzed by the stares and I couldn't move," Mary said. Then she said that the thing actually spoke to her in full sentences. In an eerie moan that rang of despair and hatred, it demanded that she pay for "the heinous heartache and damages of the whoremongers." "It yelled at me. It said that I was the 'caretaker of sorrow' and that it was the Montroses who killed its family. It said it was a slave of the house, but did not deserve to lose its loved ones because of a greedy landholder," Mary told us.

Silvana and I were extremely troubled by what we heard. But at least now we had some clues. We left Mary's, assuring her that we would be able to help, and it occurred to me that whatever had spooked Mary—even if it was her own imagination—was evidence of a link between the café and Mary's family that we could use to make sense out of this case. The use of the word *landholder* stuck in my mind. I remember reading it used as New York slang in the late eighteenth century to describe what we more commonly know as a landlord or real estate owner. When I mentioned this to Silvana, she suggested that we check the city records to see if the building that housed the Velvet Room Café had any connection to Mary's family.

Sure enough, at the New York City Building Department's Bureau of Records in Manhattan we discovered that Mary's family, the Montroses, owned quite a bit of real estate on the east side of Manhattan and from what we could discern from the old records, one of her ancestors had owned the very building plot that housed the café. After searching microfiche newspaper pages from that era, we discovered that the Montrose House, as it was called, originally a refuge for the destitute, became a "bawdy house" or brothel after its owner Murdoch Montrose evicted the shelter's operator. It was reported that Montrose tossed the tenants, who included a caretaker, his wife, and six children, into the street. After some more digging, we found newspaper accounts about the caretaker being arrested after he assaulted Murdoch in a street brawl. Apparently, some of his children died as a result of their homelessness and the caretaker went berserk. We also discovered that the caretaker was later released from jail and returned to the brothel, violently confronted Murdoch once again, and was ultimately shot dead by one of Murdoch's henchmen. The newspaper articles made it obvious that Murdoch's motivation was greed—just as the ghost had told Mary. It was also evident that Mary Montrose was now suffering from a curse levied on her ancestors over two hundred years ago. Now we knew that when Mary entered the Velvet Room Café she set the spirit off. Somehow it knew she was a blood relative and it was determined to wreak revenge. We phoned Mary immediately and told her what we uncovered about her family's involvement with the café and that if we could perform a ceremony, perhaps a séance or exorcism using Silvana as a medium, we could offer some kind of help to undo the Montrose curse and release the spirit. We thought it best to conduct the séance in the café itself, so we called the next morning to set up an appointment to visit.

The café normally opened early to cater to the breakfast crowd, but oddly enough no one answered when we called. When we tried three times later after 10:00 A.M., and there was still no answer, Silvana and I decided to ride down to see Langley for ourselves. "It will be better to talk first to him directly about matters so strange," Silvana said to me in her Czech accent.

About three blocks from the café, we were trapped in traffic, not atypical for midtown Manhattan. I didn't like the look in Silvana's eyes as our cab came to a dead stop. She turned her head toward me, but before she could utter a word I said, "Let's get out and walk." We started down the block and we could see the problem up ahead: fire trucks and emergency vehicles blocked the street. At first, I thought, hoped, that it wasn't what I suspected. But Silvana's walk, now turned into a trot, confirmed the worst. She was ahead of me yelling, "Robert, the café, it has burned down!"

We managed to find Langley, seriously distraught, and called him over to us outside of the fire lines. He said that his place had mysteriously caught fire last evening and that it had been destroyed and the building would probably have to be demolished. He rambled on about his losses and his business woes and then added, "And, oh yeah, that crazy woman was by here this morning, too. She just stared and smiled . . . nuts!"

Later, we visited Mary and were surprised to see her in good spirits. Actually, she was better than we had ever seen her. She of course knew that the café had burned down and said that she felt "relieved." "You both made me realize the heartache my ancestors were responsible for and I am truly sorry. I believe that my family's past regressions were somehow purged in the flames of the fire last night. The ghost was obviously happy that the place burned down and I feel it will never bother me again. I sincerely thank you both for your compassion and help. And of course . . . please bill me whatever the cost."

As Silvana and I turned to leave the apartment, we were happy to know that at least Mary was now satisfied that the curse had been lifted. But we couldn't explain the coincidental burning of the store just when we were about to perform the exorcism and séance. We also couldn't explain the sudden calm in Mary's demeanor. Silvana, more than I, was particularly observant about Mary's attitude and was shocked to see that Mary wasn't wearing the priceless initial "M" diamond brooch she wore constantly. She politely asked Mary where the brooch was, and Mary answered quite matter-of-factly, "Oh, I think I may have lost it . . . perhaps at the café during one of my episodes. It was much too ostentatious anyway.

It's probably burned and lost in the fire now. I won't miss it much. It's a small *price to pay* for peace of mind. Wouldn't you agree?" Mary asked, smiling.

Epilogue

The cause of the Velvet Room Café fire was never discovered, although according to New York City Fire Department records, arson was not ruled out. Langley was not a suspect and insurance fraud was ruled out because there was no obvious motive—the business was doing well.

We phoned Mary Montrose some months later and asked if her paranormal experiences were truly over. She said everything was fine and her life was completely free of any odd occurrences. She mentioned that she had contacted Langley about rebuilding on his burned-out lot. "Oddly enough," she said, "each time he planned to rebuild his business on the land, something inevitably queered the operation. It didn't surprise me, however. So, we agreed to build a community center. Langley's happy with that. He told me that he could sleep nights again. Seems he was having some difficulty," Mary said.

2.

Norma Vasquez's
Afterlife Detective

Paul Vasquez had been cheating on his wife, Norma, for nearly two years, and like most lowlifes he thought he'd never be caught—especially not by his father-in-law, who died four years before the couple had gotten married.

The young Bronx mother of three knew that Paul was having a torrid affair with another woman, ruining her marital relations and causing her family great distress. Each time Norma confronted her husband, he flatly denied any wrongdoing, and when pressed he either completely ignored her or became so agitated that Norma feared he might become violent. The situation was so out of hand that she could no longer ask him anything about his life outside of their Bronx apartment. He would flail his arms, scream at her, and throw things around their cramped apartment at the mere mention of his private life.

But Norma's accusations were not unfounded. On many occasions, she found love notes in his clothes, and he'd often stay out late and return smelling of a woman's perfume. Norma lost count of how many times the phone rang and, as soon as the other party heard her voice, there was a hang-up and a dial tone. All classic signs of philandering, albeit sloppy ones. But despite Paul's uncaring attitude toward his family, or his arrogance about being caught, he never bargained that his wife's major ally would turn out to be her father. Not so out of the ordinary one might think, but Norma's father had died of a massive heart attack before the couple had even announced their engagement. And he returned from the dead to apparently set matters straight.

Cry for Help

One Friday evening after a particularly nasty argument with Paul that left Norma bruised both physically and emotionally, in a fit of panic she ran to her closest relative in her Bronx neighborhood on East Tremont Avenue. Aunt Carmen had liked and protected Norma since she was a child in their middle-class world. Carmen knew how the other children's teasing affected little Norma, who, although slightly overweight for her age, had stunningly pretty Latin features and flawless skin. She would tell Norma not to cry about being teased and that one day she would grow up to be a beautiful woman who all of the men in the world would want to date and that she would be married to a wonderful man who would care for her for the rest of her life. But Paul, Norma's high school love and eventual husband, was not that man, and in fact was nothing but a constant source of misery to her. So Norma's cry for security once again went out to Aunt Carmen, whom she knew would make things right.

Norma was at the end of her rope when she visited Carmen that Friday evening to ask for help. She knew that Carmen was a wise woman, but she also remembered the many neighborhood stories about Carmen's "powers"—her ability to use the magic of Santería. Norma had spent hours at the neighborhood *botanica* (a store that caters to the metaphysical needs of the Hispanic community) watching her aunt console the locals with sage advice, special instructions for the use of charms and powders, and, of course, the candle magic offerings to the Catholic saints that most of the faithful knew could right almost any ill. She was sure that Carmen had a potion or candle that would help make Paul change his ways, or uncover the identify of this other woman was who was running her family life. She could at least then confront that woman and find some closure.

And Carmen didn't disappoint her niece. She provided Norma with her strongest talismans and mixtures. She used the reading of animal parts and bones as she performed her most powerful candle magic, offering many devotions to the particular saints known to help in overcoming family and marital problems. But nothing worked. Paul continued to play around, Norma was abused, and their children suffered. Carmen told Norma she had one last chance: "We must ask for help from the other side, my child. We must seek the advice of the dead—they can see all on this earth. You must ask them or your life will continue in pain. It is your only resort."

The Haunted Husband

Our telephone rang at X-Investigations just before 7:00 P.M. on the Wednesday before Thanksgiving holiday of 1999. Silvana, my Czech assistant, had already left for the weekend and I was gathering the paperwork I was planning to look over during the holiday to prepare for my lecture on using occult magic in the business world at the Borough of Manhattan Community College the following week. I hurried to answer the phone in hopes that it was a telemarketer so that I could begin my holiday. But Carmen Garcia's urgent plea in broken Spanish to assist her and her niece using the "eyes of the dead" was too intriguing and fascinating to blow off for another turkey day. "This is X-Investigations?" Carmen asked after a moment. "You are knowledgeable about the afterlife and how we can summon the dead to help us?"

It was a good thirty seconds before I could get a word in edgewise. Carmen at least let me answer that this was in fact X-Investigations, but the moment I said that I understood her plea, she cut me short and began to ramble about her niece Norma's domestic predicament and that they had exhausted all known regular and magical aids. I managed to discover that they wanted to conduct a séance to contact someone that Norma trusted to help uncover why Norma's husband, Paul, was cheating on her and with whom. "It is very important to my niece and her children that we take care of this problem soon," Carmen said. "I have used all of my magical knowledge, but nothing is working for us."

I laid down my briefcase and sat back in my chair, resigning myself to the fact that I wasn't going anywhere this

Thanksgiving eve. I discussed at length Carmen's knowledge of the occult, especially the ways of Santería, and what spells, talismans, and so on she had tried to overcome Norma's problem. Carmen was indeed an expert in the ways of her craft, citing ancient tribal remedies and ceremonies that I knew were authentic from my prior research into the field. She told me of the orishas—the gods of Santería—and the offerings she sacrificed to them. She also hinted at the ways of Voodoun and the necromantic powers of controlling the dead. But what struck me most was how defeated Carmen sounded. She was obviously concerned with her niece's welfare, but she was also frightened of something else. I later discovered that Carmen had a twofold reason for wanting to conduct the séance that involved her own occult powers as well as Norma's requests. This made the case that much more interesting to me, so I decided on the spot that X-Investigations would assist Carmen and her niece in their attempt to contact the "other side." What I didn't bargain for was that my decision would put Silvana's and my sanity in jeopardy—and our lives in danger.

I asked Silvana to call on Norma the Friday after Thanksgiving at her home in the Bronx. I thought talking to another woman would make Norma feel more comfortable in this delicate situation. Silvana expected to meet with a worried mother and wife, but she didn't expect to see and hear the strange occurrences in the apartment. The interview began normally with the standard questions and answers. We typically ask about any religious beliefs, mental illness, superstitions, and so on, so we can weed out any preconceived prejudices the subject might have regarding our work. Silvana then asked Norma why she had requested a séance, since there are many regular investigative techniques available to nab a philandering husband. Or Norma could have opted to use our regular clairvoyant means of tapping into unknown realms. But Norma reminded Silvana that Aunt Carmen had tried all of her magical skills to no avail.

Then, curiously enough, Norma became reticent and just stopped in the middle of the conversation. "What is wrong, Norma?" Silvana asked.

Norma raised her head and in a teary voice said, "Very strange things are happening here. It is my father, who died many years ago. He comes into my room at night when I am sleeping and he is very angry with me. He always hated Paul and now he is punishing me for Paul's lustful behavior. I am very frightened. His cold hands touch me and the dark closes in on me." At that very moment, Norma began to scream and clutch at her chest. "Ay, Dios mio! My neck, the marks are coming again!"

Silvana was stunned to see stigmatalike welts rising on Norma's skin right above her breasts. The welts looked like finger marks squeezing the flesh. "He does not want me to talk to you. He doesn't want you to help me. My father is very angry because I did not heed his warnings about Paul when he was alive."

After Silvana calmed Norma, she called me on her cell phone. She recounted what had just happened and said that Norma not only wanted to contact her dead father for help, but also that she needed to be released from his ghostly grip. Norma was haunted on earth by her husband's misdeeds and by her father's spirit. "Robert, we must act quickly or Norma will become possessed. I felt a very powerful presence in the room with us. It is deep and very angry with anyone near Norma. She is in danger. We also will be in danger. You must know this before we begin," Silvana said in her heavy east European accent. I told her we would discuss it further in the office and asked if she was safe at the moment. "He knows I am clairvoyant . . . this one knows I can reach him and force him to come to us. He has touched me already, Robert," Silvana said in a disturbingly unfamiliar voice. I could tell that she was very worried.

We later learned that there were other strange things happening at Norma's apartment. Personal items always related to Norma and Paul's marriage were missing, pictures of the family would mysteriously develop spots or be blown off of the mantel, and Norma's engagement ring simply disappeared. But the strangest of all was Norma's recounting of the last time she had sex with Paul. She said it was normal intercourse—Paul had never been a very considerate lover and was prone to jumping on Norma in a missionary position and stroking until just *he* was satisfied. But this night, at the very moment when he entered her, Norma oddly took notice of the old 8x10 black-and-white photo of her mother and father on her bureau. She said her father's face seemed to enlarge at first as Paul pushed and then exploded off of the photo as Paul entered her. The giant face shot out of the photo like a Hollywood special effect with bulging red eyes and sweating brow. The gruesome head undulated and circled the room, eyes peering down at the couple, mouth slobbering and spewing forth vile comments that only Norma could hear. Although embarrassed at the bizarre tale, Norma forced herself to explain to us how her vagina began to burn as though some caustic chemical had been poured into her. The more Paul pushed, the more she burned from the inside. The entity screamed at Norma, "You are getting what you deserve. He is evil. He will burn your soul!" Norma put her head down as she told the story and cupped her face in her hands, frightened and near the end of her rope.

We knew we had to help, but I was troubled by the facts, or I should say the lack thereof. Things just didn't add up in my mind. Carmen's magic hadn't helped, yet she wanted us to conduct a séance, something she would have certainly been prepared to do herself considering her occult prowess. And Norma's father, with whom she had had a good relationship until Paul's arrival, was turning into a malevolent haunting that was seeking to harm the young wife. And yet, both women wanted *us* to conduct a séance to contact Norma's father and help indict the husband. Something was fishy in spook world.

When I mentioned my concerns to Silvana, she said that I was the "occult expert" and that she was only the medium. "I can *feel* things Robert, but you must do the brain work," she said.

"Well, what did you feel about the two women? Anything out of the ordinary?" I asked.

Silvana shot back almost flippantly, "Oh yes, the dead, they already speak to Carmen about this problem." "What?!" I was surprised that Silvana hadn't mentioned this before, but then this was our first real analysis of the case and I had to admit that I was preoccupied by Norma's grief over the damage to her family life. But Silvana's comment raised further suspicions about the women's request. It also sparked an idea: we would conduct a séance under the guise of wanting to contact the deceased father. Silvana could use her clairvoyant powers to "feel" Carmen's association with the afterlife and perhaps give us a clue as to the real motives behind the séance request.

The Séance

The following Friday evening when Silvana and I arrived at Norma's apartment, the statues of at least a dozen Catholic saints were eerily illuminated by tall red and yellow candles in glass containers on the kitchen table. The flickering flames lent the statues' faces the illusion of expression. A fitting atmosphere, I thought, for the "other world" events that were about to unfold. Norma offered us refreshments but we were eager to get right to work. Our group assumed the standard séance positions, holding hands in a circle around the kitchen table. The room was dark except for the candlelight and there was a faint odor of breakfast cooking mixed with the smoky scent of the candles. Supermarket candles such as these typically don't have cotton wicks and tend to give off a distinctive odor. I often "pick up" on odors in our cases as a regular investigative technique. In the past, I was able to "smell evil," so to speak, and I'm acutely attuned to any odor out of the ordinary.

Silvana prepared for her trance by bowing her head and placing her chin down against her chest while laying her hands flat on the table in front of her. I could see Norma and Carmen glance at each other with a look of apprehension. At first, I wasn't sure whether their glance indicated nervousness or fear. Although the two women thought we were about to contact Norma's father, our real motive was to discover whether Carmen was already in touch with the spirit world and if so—and more important—why?

Silvana drifted slowly into her trance. We were instructed by her before the séance to quietly chant the words "Miguel" and "Junior," Norma's father's name and nickname, in rhythm, almost humming. We began the chant and within seconds Norma's eyes began to water. I could see that she was becoming agitated and frightened, yet Carmen was curiously distracted, peering over at Norma repeatedly and then looking at me. The air was clogged with fear and anticipation. The odor changed from the Bronx apartment familiar to that of something like spoiled milk. We were about to touch another realm of reality. It wasn't in our minds. We could see it, touch it, and smell it. It was real—and we all knew it.

Silvana's body became rigid in the metal kitchen chair and her dark eyes rolled back into her head, exposing only white orbs that shone like large marbles. Her skin turned waxen and pale, almost translucent, while guttural grunts and moans erupted from deep within her chest. The sounds bothered me. I had seen Silvana in séances before, but these sounds were like those of someone hurt or in distress. My impulse was to shake her out of the trance, but I was committed to finishing our job, no matter how disturbing.

After a few moments, Silvana raised her head and began to speak. We expected to hear a male voice, that of Norma's father Miguel, who would cross over and speak to us. But we were shocked when Silvana spoke to us in her own voice. She said, "I cannot contact the spirit you seek. The witch Carmen has conducted necromantic blasphemies; the guardians will not allow the tortured one to communicate his true words." Before we could respond, Carmen stood up, breaking our circle, and ran out the front door of the apartment. Norma stood and yelled after her, "Aunt Carmen, what is wrong? What is the matter?" Then she turned to me and asked, "I don't understand what is happening. Why did my aunt leave? What does this all mean? Is my aunt evil? Is she an evil witch?" Sobbing pitifully, Norma asked one question after another.

Silvana released herself from her trance and rested her head in her hands. Her blouse was wet with sweat but the color was returning to her face. I asked if she was all right and she nodded as she grasped my wrist. "Robert. I have found our problem. Carmen has done black magic with the dead. She wants to make Miguel her slave on earth. I feel she has chained his spirit to do her bidding." I was shocked, but what Silvana was saying explained why Carmen had bolted. I wasn't aware of any Santería spells that would bind ghosts, but Santería is a close relative of vodoun, and there was a possibility that Carmen was an evil sorceress in disguise—a *boko*. I remembered her mentioning vodoun in passing during our earlier discussions. I then suspected that Carmen could have conducted *kou nanm*, a soul spell, to capture Miguel's spirit, or worse, she could have conducted a *voye lamo* spell, one that sends a dead spirit to inhabit a victim.

I asked Silvana to stay at the table because I wanted her to enter her trance state again, this time without Carmen in the room. I asked Norma to indulge us, despite her anxiety, explaining that I might obtain some important answers to her problems. The young woman, now exhausted from the ritual, could only moan, "Yes, yes. Do what you will."

We once again began the ritual, me holding hands with Norma as Silvana crossed over. This time, Silvana was more relaxed and in control, but when she began to speak my suspicions were confirmed. This time, her voice was that of Miguel's. Norma's entire body shook and once again she began to cry as she heard the voice of her father speaking to us. "That is him! That is my father," Norma shrieked.

To those who have never experienced a legitimate séance, the presence in the room is indescribable. It's not simply a familiar voice or a shadowy movement. A pressure in the air begins to surround the table and the darkness expands around the participants. This episode was no different—except for the tears. Not Norma's this time, but the tears of her father. Silvana's ghostly voice began to speak to Norma directly . . . Norma stood up at the table, her hands shaking as Silvana spoke. "My little sparrow, I am with you always. But there is bad magic causing me to say and do things that I would never do. I have been the cause of all of your pain. Paul is also a victim. Find it in your heart to forgive him," the voice within Silvana said. Then the strangest phenomena of the evening occurred. Norma stood up and water . . . tears, began to fall onto her outstretched hands, dripping onto the table and glistening in the glow from the candles. There was no leak in the ceiling and her hands were extended too far from her body to have become wet from her own tears. Norma's father's tears were falling from beyond, touching the woman's skin . . . and her heart.

When this part of the séance ended, Silvana and I immediately knew we had hit pay dirt. We looked at each other acknowledging what we had just experienced. Carmen, Norma's aunt, had manipulated the spirit of Miguel through vodoun magic and bound him with her power. This explained why none of Carmen's supposed magic had worked to expose Paul's indiscretions. It had all been a diversion to trick

Norma. When Miguel's spirit asked Norma to forgive Paul, we reasoned that Carmen had forced Miguel's spirit to possess Paul and possibly turn him into the philanderer who was ruining Norma's life. Carmen knew that she could control Miguel through Paul. He could be a cheating husband or he could be a murderer. What could be worse for a father, even a departed one, than to be the tool to cause his child's pain? There was only one thing left for us to do: release Miguel's soul from Carmen's vodoun grip, but it could be dangerous.

The Exorcism

Because we knew Carmen would not cooperate, claiming we were charlatans and simply out to steal Norma's money, we had to resort to our own knowledge of vodoun curses and spells to counteract Carmen's black magic. Fortunately, Norma believed we had her best interests at heart and at this point distrusted her aunt. There are a number of ways that a boko can arrest the spirit of the dead, but I decided that we would attempt to release him by reversing the usual and typical methods used by the bokos. Traditionally, the sorcerer will contract or "buy" an evil vodoun god or *Lwa* with sacrifices and offerings. This becomes an *angajan* or engagement for life—a powerful agreement that the sorcerer knows can never be broken voluntarily. The bokos will do almost anything to prevent the pact from being broken. In the case of summoning the dead, the boko will also conjure the assistance of the god Baron Samedi, the expediter of the dead, and offer gifts to the saint associated with Samedi. An awesome amount of skill, ceremony, and sacrifice are called for to control the dead. I knew we were up against a strong sorceress, and we were well aware that breaking the spell would be dangerous. Bokos are adept at throwing curses on their enemies in the form of evil spells, charms, and even unleashing demonic monsters—so we were prepared for the worst.

The first step in our plan was to contact the Lwa Kafou, the godfather of vodoun black magic, and bind him to our will. We didn't know what god Carmen made her deal with, but we knew Kafou could influence all other evil entities. If we could control Kafou, we could release Miguel's spirit. We also had to protect Norma. We decided to use the traditional method of protection by creating a *gad*, a vodoun charm that Norma could wear during the séance. The gad is usually prepared in the form of a tattoo drawn with the sign of a saint that is meant to protect the wearer from evil. It is applied as a paste made from herbal powders obtained at local botanicas. I also contacted a colleague, a professor of anthropology at New York University who is an expert in Haitian vodoun. I recalled that he had recorded actual vodoun ritual drumming and I asked if I could borrow the chants to use as a backdrop sound. Using the drums would enhance our ritual setting and help Silvana enter the proper trance state.

We then headed to St. John's Cemetery in Queens, New York, where Miguel was buried. The cemetery is not easily accessible—especially at midnight. But it's where we had to go to get the necessary grave dirt required in the ritual to summon Baron Samedi and gain entrée to the Lwa Kafou. The only good thing about the evil Lwa is that they can be bought—with gifts and sacrifices. And although they usually require lifelong devotion, the "right price," usually in the form of information about a boko with whom they already do business, can sway them to do your bidding. Norma agreed that we could reveal that Carmen was a Santería priestess—a "conflict of interests" for a vodoun boko and something the Lwa Kafou could use to keep Carmen loyal to him for the rest of her life.

We managed to enter the cemetery through a bent gate on the main access road off Metropolitan Avenue. Although Norma had given us the exact location of Miguel's grave, finding the spot in such a large cemetery at night with just a flashlight was quite a chore—and potentially a criminal act. Silvana was complaining of the cold (she always opts to dress sexy rather than warm)—I was more concerned about "disturbing the dead." But we both agreed that the excursion was creepy, and the sooner we got out of there, the better.

After an hour of misdirection, we finally found Miguel's grave deep inside the cemetery's center plots. Silvana and I cleared the dead leaves that covered the headstone and began our work. We dug a small hole at the foot of the headstone. The ground was surprisingly soft for early December in New York City, so we were able to dig deep enough to get the requisite grave dirt from at least a foot down. I dug the hole wide enough to insert my hand and thrust it into the damp earth. As I fished around, I was pleasantly surprised to smell the fresh earth, not decay, and I envisioned Miguel's spirit smiling at our work. When my arm was into the grave up to my elbow, I grabbed a handful of dirt and brought it to the surface, half-expecting a corpse's hand to grab for me. Silvana was pleading with me to hurry, again complaining about the wind and concerned that we would be caught. The cold night winds were indeed blowing all through our adventure, but the second I had the dirt at the surface and deposited into our plastic baggie, the wind suddenly stopped and the night became calm. Silvana's mood suddenly changed and she said calmly, "Miguel's spirit is pleased."

Our exorcism began the very next evening. Norma, Silvana, and I were again seated at Norma's kitchen table. The procedure was to anoint Norma with the protective gad, summon Baron Samedi, and ask him for entrée to Lwa Kafou, whom we would bind to do our bidding by offering him knowledge of Carmen's dual allegiances.

With the vodoun drum music in the background, we prepared Norma for the ritual by having her read a standard Catholic prayer bought from the local botanica and written specifically for Saint Radegonde, the counterpart of Samedi. As she recited the words in the prayer over and over, "Protect me, holy saint, protect me from the dark and evil that manifests itself in hell," we mixed the special herb powders into the paste that's used to paint the protective tattoo. Norma continued to recite the prayer as we painted the *vever* or magical sign of Samedi on her arm. Norma was apprehensive, remembering the trauma she had felt at our last meeting, but she realized the exorcism had to be done.

Silvana was no stranger to vodoun ritual, having spent years in Haiti as a research assistant, so she knew how to enter the special altered state required to be the conduit to contact Kafou. I reminded her that if she sensed any trouble she should exit the state immediately. I suspected that Carmen was casting spells against us, so if we let our guard down and became vulnerable, the spirits could enter our lives and wreak havoc. Silvana nodded to me, closed her eyes, and entered her trance state within seconds with the help of the pounding drum recordings.

With Norma's protective gad complete and Silvana in her trance, we were ready to contact Samedi. I offered traditional sweets and wines to Samedi as ice-breaking booty until I was sure Silvana had made the connection. The drums continued and although Norma was protected she appeared to be in a trance as well, focusing on the ceiling of her kitchen and swaying to the beat of the drums. I was the only one in the room at this point who was in a normal state of consciousness and I realized that I had to overcome any fears of the unknown in order to complete our work. I felt fine until Silvana began to groan.

My partner now had Samedi's spirit within her. And although what was coming from her mouth were not words, I could tell by her contorted body movements that she was truly possessed. I immediately offered Samedi the gifts and asked him to hear Norma's prayers and put us in contact with Kafou—the king of evil vodoun gods. Silvana continued to writhe in the chair, uttering undecipherable sounds. I asked Samedi repeatedly to answer our request. Norma was now writhing along with Silvana as the room became disturbingly hot and humid. I was sweating profusely, although the apartment heat was turned off and the outside temperature was well below 40 degrees. The rhythm of the drums and the women swaying nearly made me swoon, but I managed to maintain my composure and relentlessly pressed Samedi to give us what we needed. All at once the music stopped (the machine was still rolling). Silvana straightened in her chair and my jaw dropped as I saw a black bilelike drool leak from her mouth as she whispered, "Who dares summon Kafou?"

My hands were shaking and I felt very alone. I knew the only protection I had from the spirit world was my knowledge of how to manipulate evil entities. Any curse Carmen had thrown would be nothing compared to what could have happened to my mind and soul if this exorcism failed. I challenged Kafou immediately, saying that I was aware of his boko Carmen and that I had information about her that he needed. Silvana asked, "What is this knowledge?"

I managed to gather my courage and said I would tell only if he would release Miguel, Norma's father, from his boko's command. There was no response. But within seconds Norma rose from her chair and moved toward Silvana. I was shocked to see her then kiss Silvana passionately on the mouth, turn around, and sit back in her chair as if nothing happened. After the initial shock wore off, I realized it was Kafou's way of "feeling" Norma's soul so he would know her as Miguel's blood relation. It was my sign that he agreed to our arrangement.

I then explained to the entity of Kafou, through Silvana's trance, just what Carmen had done, and shortly thereafter, with all three of us totally spent from the episode, I ended the ceremony. Silvana was so exhausted she actually lost consciousness for almost ten minutes. Norma said that she had fallen asleep, not recalling the kiss or even Silvana speaking to us at all. She simply asked if everything was all right. I told her we had reached the other side and it was now in the hands of the vodoun gods and, of course, her father.

Epilogue

Silvana and I were pleased to hear from Norma a few weeks later on Christmas Eve. She sounded exuberant and calm, mentioning that she, Paul, and the kids were looking forward to a wonderful Christmas Day. She politely asked me about the fee for our services, but I said we could talk about it after the holidays. She then explained that Paul was in the room with her and that she just wanted to thank us for our help. She added that there was "a remarkable change" in his behavior. "He is playing with the children right now and tomorrow we are having a large family dinner," Norma said. I couldn't help but ask if Carmen was going to be present at the gathering. "Well, no," Norma said. "We have heard that Aunt Carmen has left town. We think she has gone on vacation to Haiti for the holidays . . . or perhaps longer."

3.

The Transylvanian Curse

Petrov and Anna Sighisoura were the parents of a sixteen-year-old boy. They lived in suburban Stratford, Connecticut, a middle-class town known for its ethnic mix. Their son, Charles, was an average teenager for the better part of his youth. He was a good student and was interested in girls, sports, and, of course, every video game he could get his hands on, especially anything to do with role-playing of the Dungeons and Dragons variety. And his parents indulged his fantasies despite the fact that he spent too much time on the computer and at the local comic book store playing the games and discussing the intricacies of spells and demons with his friends. Even the occasional brooding after losing one of the role-playing games and the bursts of anger directed at his peers who bested him at the latest bout were tolerated by Petrov and Anna. Nothing seemed out of the ordinary. And despite Anna's dedication to her Russian Orthodox religion, and its strict proscription against delving into anything "occult" or magical, Anna even cast a blind eye toward Charles's latest obsession with "vampire" role-playing games.

Despite his occult leanings, Charles pleased his parents. Petrov was particularly happy when Charles turned sixteen, the customary age that ushered a boy into manhood in Petrov and Anna's hometown of Sighisoura, Romania (the name they chose for their surname in America), in Transylvania. This marked the beginning of great things for Charles in Petrov's mind: independence, career planning, thoughts of a family, religious commitment, and most of all learning the history and secret code of the family that was the creed by which all its men lived. It was a blood oath of sorts that bonded each male member of the family forever. The oath had been created centuries ago in the ranks of the warring armies of Romania as they fought the Roman legions. The blood oath was as sacred as any religious teaching or doctrine and was far more revered and equally feared because of the claim that the blood oath had been forged to protect the family from dark forces of nature. If the blood oath was not followed to the letter, great misery would befall them. If it was desecrated in any way, a family would be cursed forever to a "living death." Petrov was elated by Charles's birthday, but his joy soon turned to terror when he learned that his son had blasphemously perverted the family's blood oath and may even have suffered the "living death" by becoming a vampire.

The Goth Problem

According to Petrov and Anna, the trouble began when Charles became involved in the local Goth scene in Stratford. They tolerated the role-playing gaming and the many

afternoons and evenings Charles and his friends whiled away
the hours playing and discussing the battles and magical
incantations they were using against each other to gain victory. The role-playing then switched to a game they said was
called "The Gathering," where clans of vampires competed
with each other in life-or-death struggles that included horrific acts of brutality and many blasphemies. Anna recounted
how she cringed one evening when learning that Charles was
planning on decapitating one of his rivals. "I knew it was just
a game, but the way Charles described it to his friend with all
of the gory details—severing the head just below the Adam's
apple so the artery would gush blood in the quickest
manner—well, it was too much for me to handle. I screamed
at him, 'Charles, that is disgusting talk. God does not want to
hear that from your mouth even if it's a game.' It disturbed
me to no end when Charles said, 'Mom, God has no place in
this world.'"

The vampire role-playing quickly expanded between
Charles and his peers. The boys began to dress in all black
Victorian Gothic clothing, often wearing pale makeup and
painting their fingernails black. Although it was quite disturbing to the Sighisouras, they believed that Charles was a
good boy at heart and was participating in faddish behavior
with his friends, as do most adolescent boys. The group that
called itself "The Brooding," began as a Friday-evening game-
playing gathering at one of the boys' houses. When Charles
hadn't requested that the Brooding use the Sighisouras' house
for over two months, Petrov became suspicious and asked
Charles where his game meetings were being held. Charles
confessed that the game playing was over and that the group
was now hanging out at a local teen Goth club. "He said to

me, 'Dad, there are girls there. That's more fun than games now.' I couldn't argue that point with a sixteen-year-old boy. I thought it was fine and healthy, despite his crazy clothing," Petrov said.

But Anna had deep and disturbing reservations about her son's new behavior. She was always more attuned to her son's demeanor, something she attributed to her "gypsy sight"— an uncanny ability to sense both good and evil manifestations in relatives and close friends. And, of course, being Charles's mother alerted Anna even more to a strange feeling she received from her son in the last few months. She described it as a morose, black shadow that was seeping into his spirit. When I asked Anna if she could give me an example of her impression, she said that it was as "if the light of Charles's soul is being slowly extinguished like an eclipse of the sun. A giant blackness is shadowing my boy. I've become more frightened every day. I pray that it is just my imagination, but it is much too strong and it is getting stronger. I had to tell Petrov, it has become so bad. I am very, very frightened," Anna said.

Her fears were not unfounded. Anna began to find Charles's soiled shirts spotted with what looked like blood. First, there were just small round droplet stains that she discounted as perhaps some cherry juice or other fruit stain. But when the spots became larger and had the distinct deep dark red, almost black color of human blood, Anna became alarmed. She became so obsessed with the increasing bloodstains that she literally tore apart Charles's room one afternoon to inspect all of his belongings. Anna searched every drawer, his closet, under his bed, each shelf, and even went through his boxes of magazines and books. What she found was at first more curious than disturbing. Anna discovered a silver box she had never seen before that looked antique and was inscribed with strange symbols. She opened it cautiously and was perplexed to see that it was filled with rich, black earth, the kind you might get from a plant nursery, dense and black, not at all the type found in the back yards of most local homes. And the instant she opened the box, she noticed an alarming odor she could only describe as the smell of decay and death, very old and musty, yet at the same time mixed with a human scent. She also swore that she saw bone fragments mixed in with the earth. She felt a chill run down her spine as her "gypsy sight" tingled. She told me that she felt the darkness once again that she knew was enveloping her son.

Anna decided not to confront Charles with the mysterious box until she first spoke with Petrov. When her husband retuned home from work that evening, he could see that Anna was troubled. "It was that 'gypsy' look in her eyes that told me she experienced something very bad," Petrov said. Anna told Petrov of her morbid discovery and he quickly blurted out that the change in Charles had occurred right after their discussion of the family blood oath. He recounted that Charles was fascinated with the rituals and the mythos of the oath, but at the same time questioned its validity. Charles had said that the darkness wasn't always a bad place and that there was great power in the unseen. "He said to me that our heritage often spoke of vampires and their immortality. He thought it would be 'very cool' to live forever, at any cost!" Petrov dismissed his son's comments at the time, all the while knowing they could mean trouble. He warned Charles about the blood oath and gave him the sacred instructions to carry out in privacy. "I warned him not to change the ritual at all or, God forbid, do anything to disgrace or blaspheme it. I told him there is great power in it for good and evil. When I said that, he smiled, so I assumed everything was fine."

But when he heard from Anna about the box of earth—a key element of using the blood oath's powers for evil gain—Petrov was shocked. He told her to get the box immediately and dispose of it. Petrov realized that Charles was using the secrets of the oath for his own gain and, coupled with his new friends, weird clothing, and Anna's concern over the blood on Charles's shirt, Petrov recognized all of the telltale historical signs of attempts to use the blood oath to satisfy the lust for power and riches. He had had a long talk with Charles about the oath and was pleased by his son's earnest interest. Charles seemed genuinely excited about its history, the effects it had on the binding of the males of the family, and especially its mysterious powers. Petrov didn't think it was odd for Charles to ask so many questions, even considering that most of them centered on the oath's ability to grant power. He even dismissed Charles's most obviously excited question as boyhood exuberance for the fantastic when he asked, "Papa, you mean I can become immortal?"

But after Anna's alarming discoveries, Petrov feared the worst. He felt that the ancient curse was about to befall the Sighisoura family. A curse that he could not control without help from both this world—and the supernatural.

Curses

The first celebrity interview I ever conducted was back in the 1970s with renowned Dracula hunter Dr. Raymond McNally, author of *In Search of Dracula*. It was fascinating to learn that the legends and myths of vampires, especially in Romania and the region of Transylvania, were largely based on fact. McNally was the first to make public the story of the Romanian ruler and conqueror Vlad Tepes, also known as Vlad the Impaler, as the archetype for the mythical vampire Dracula. At the same time, he didn't discount factual vampirism, or at the very least the belief and the psychological results of the belief in vampires.

When the opportunity arose to take a pleasurable "Dracula tour" vacation to the heart of Transylvania to explore the history of the world's most famous monster, I jumped at the chance. My trip was booked well in advance and I looked forward to being able to relax and study the Dracula legend as a total indulgence without the pressures of business. But my hopes were short lived. A friend and colleague, Dr. Brad Schultz, a social service psychologist in New York City, called me one evening while I was sitting contentedly in front of my apartment fireplace and thumbing through the travel brochures. "Brad, good to hear from you. I was just looking at the materials on my trip to Transylvania—it's going to be great. I can't wait to go."

Brad said that it was a coincidence that I had mentioned the trip because he had just had an interesting visit from a local couple that had family in the region. I didn't think it was much of a coincidence until Brad began telling me of the Sighisouras' visit with him and their dilemma. He said that they had no one to turn to about the problem with Charles, and because they had visited with him before about a minor problem with Charles's adjustment to high school, they were comfortable with Brad and felt he could be trusted. Even though their new problem was far from anything Brad had dealt with before, the couple was desperate for help of any kind.

Brad went on for the better part of an hour, explaining the story of the Sighisoura family's blood oath and their problem with Charles. I was fascinated and as Brad spoke I knew that my "pleasure" trip to Transylvania would soon be mixed with business of a most blood-chilling kind. I agreed to help the concerned couple and told Brad to have them see me prepared with everything germane to the "curse."

The Sighisouras visited my office the very next day just around noon. Considering it was a cold November day, I was surprised to see that they were dressed only in very light outerwear. "We are used to the cold. In our country, it is usually dark and rainy and very cold," Anna said. I thought to myself that now my vacation wouldn't only be mixed with business, but that I'd freeze my butt off as well. But duty called and I listened intently.

Anna and Petrov explained that they believed Charles was using the rituals of the blood oath, particularly the mixing of blood and "dead earth," or cemetery earth, together and calling on the dark forces for power and revenge. They recounted Charles's transition from a "normal" boy to one obsessed with dark role-playing and odd clothing. The bloodstained shirts were their real concern. The parents felt that Charles was delving into a dangerous world and if he perverted the blood oath, the ancient curse would ruin his life and perhaps condemn his immortal soul. There was only one solution: someone would have to visit the town of Sighisoura in Transylvania, meet with a relative of the family who had the "gypsy sight," and perform the necessary ritual to reverse Charles's actions. I asked why they couldn't have simply writ-

ten a letter or telephoned a relative to have the ritual performed. Why was it necessary to ask a perfect stranger to
travel halfway around the world? "Because to reverse the
ritual," Petrov said, "Charles must be present himself in the
homeland and we cannot afford to send him there—and he
would, of course, resist. The only alternative is to have him
take the blood oath with someone here and that person can
then seek the gypsy in Romania."

"So you want me to be Charles's proxy for the ritual in
Transylvania?" I asked.

Petrov nodded. He mentioned that it was a simple ritual
and there was not "very much bloodletting" to bind with
Charles. To me, *any* bloodletting was too much, but by that
time I was hooked on X-Investigations' first international case.

As I boarded the plane bound for Bucharest, I recalled the
ritual that had subsequently taken place in the Sighisouras'
apartment. We fabricated a story about how I was a long-
lost relative who never participated in the blood oath and
Charles was the only person in the United States who was
"fresh" enough to transfer the rite to a new member.
Charles accepted the ruse, thinking, I'm sure, that any
knowledge of the rituals and their power would benefit
him in the long run, so there was no resistance. In fact,
the only glitch was from me—when it called for us to cut
our left wrists with a ceremonial dagger and meld the dripping blood "blood brother-style" into both of our arms, I
was the one who became a bit squeamish. But the squea-
mishness wasn't the worst part. I also had an odd feeling of
dread, especially when I raised my head and saw Charles
staring intently into my eyes as the blood was exchanged.
He stared at me with a very discomforting hunger in his

eyes, almost pushing me to the point of telling the Sighisouras that they should find themselves a new investigator. I knew at that moment that this was no ordinary "psychodrama" ceremony—it was the real deal.

Transylvania

I couldn't let on to my tour group that I had a dual purpose for visiting Transylvania. Most of the other twenty-five or so members were garden-variety horror fans or looking for a different "kick." Truth is, they probably wouldn't have believed me anyway if I told them that I was on a mission to find a Romanian who could reverse a curse. And since I had originally planned the trip to be a pleasure jaunt, faking it wouldn't be that difficult. What *was* difficult was recalling the look in Charles's eyes. It creeped me out just thinking about it. I knew that unless I got past it, the feeling would haunt me on the entire flight across the Atlantic. What's more, I didn't have Silvana, my partner and comrade, to aid me on this trip. She had left just days before my call from Brad to participate in a special symposium at the Rhine Research Center for the paranormal at Duke University. It was also unfortunate for me because Silvana could have communicated more easily with the east European locals. And she has a knack for sensing trouble—an ability that has saved our hides more times than I can recall.

After arriving in Bucharest, I asked Danny, our tour guide, if he could arrange a local guide to help me find some of my relatives in the town of Sighisoura. He looked at me strangely

and asked if I knew that that town was the alleged birthplace
of Vlad the Impaler, better known as Dracula? I nodded and
quickly said, "Oh, sure. That's what makes this trip so excit-
ing for me—because I'll have a chance to ask my relations
whether the legend is true."

Danny found me a personal guide, a wiry, swarthy fellow
named Stosh, who wore a New York Mets baseball cap and
spoke a style of English that left out most conjunctions.
"Dracula born here. I take," were Stosh's first words to me. It
took the better part of an hour to explain that I needed to
visit Ilana Kastanavolksch, the Sighisouras' gypsy aunt. I
learned that Ilana lived far on the outskirts of Sighisoura,
some fifteen miles away. Stosh said that we could take his car
only so far because the road ended. I wasn't prepared for the
last leg of the journey to Ilana's house, which required us to
hitchhike on a local peasant's horse-drawn wagon through the
woods and finally through a local cemetery—the only pass-
able routes. This journey was becoming more and more
bizarre. And it may have been my mind playing tricks on me,
but the closer we got to Ilana's home, the more intense were
my memories of Charles's eyes as we performed the ritual
back in New York.

The ride to Ilana's was straight out of *Bram Stoker's Dracula*—the road, if you could call it that, was coarse, dirty, and
filled with small ravines and ditches that made New York
City's Brooklyn/Queens Expressway seem like the autobahn.
I was awed at how perfect Hollywood had been in re-creating
the Transylvanian woods—just as I remembered them from
countless horror movies. Winding passages topped in ground
fog and illuminated by a pale yellow Moon that dipped in and
out from behind twisted trees that blocked the light. And it

was cold. I turned up my collar to brace against that biting, damp cold that "goes right through you."

We had been riding in the wagon for about a half hour longer than I had anticipated. Just as I was about to ask Stosh where the hell we were, the driver said something to Stosh in the local Romanian dialect that I could tell meant we were at our destination and he wanted some money. I gave Stosh some cash and as he paid the wagon driver he pointed to Ilana's house, which was barely visible about one hundred yards ahead. As we walked over the dirt, I kept asking myself why I had taken on this assignment. Being in the "land of monsters" was surreal enough, but dealing with the supernatural in spook central started to unnerve even me. I wished that Silvana was with me to offer her usual moral support, but more important, for her experience. She would have been able to "sense" any danger that lay ahead. Although I had none of Silvana's cognitive psychic abilities, I did feel uneasy. There was an aura of something ancient and heavy in the wooded area outside Ilana's house. And the makeshift graveyard with scattered headstones and wooden crosses that lined the path only added to my suspicions. I couldn't have created a more perfect movie set in my mind, the only thing missing was the creature jumping out of the woods. But as we reached Ilana's front door and knocked, I discovered something even more frightening.

A young man answered the door. At first, I wasn't sure if I was experiencing some wicked déjà vu or if I was tired from my exhausting trip, but when the boy who answered the door came closer in the light of the Moon, I stepped back and stared at his face. This was Charles! Or Charles's twin. This young man was the exact duplicate of the boy in New York whose parents feared him cursed. This freaky coincidence instantly renewed my interest in the case and started me to think that there actually may have been more of a link to the blood oath than even Petrov understood. My mind raced as Stosh explained to the boy who we were and why we were at his front door. Maybe this boy was somehow psychically linked to Charles. Was he cursed as well? Was he *really* a vampire?

Once Ilana was convinced that I was in fact an emissary from her relative in the States, she introduced me to her son, Stephen, who appeared to be a normal teenager who was typically curious but "too cool" to show any exuberance over my arrival. I thought that the Yankees yearbook that I happened to have in my briefcase might be a good ice breaker. I had noticed that the wagon driver wore a Mets cap, as did Stosh, so I figured an American baseball item might be a good way to win over Stephen. But this boy was much more interested in my occult experiences than baseball. He asked his mother in Romanian if I had ever witnessed the living dead. As he uttered the words, Ilana made the sign of the cross three times and admonished Stephen for his blasphemy. He simply smiled and looked my way with the same disturbing eyes as Charles's.

Stephen then burst into a fit of anger when Ilana admonished him. He yelled and threw things around the small house. The intensity and suddenness of Stephen's violent outburst was startling. The teenager had become a raving beast. As clichéd as it sounds, the only way to describe Stephen's behavior was that of a man possessed. He stomped out of the kitchen where we had all met and slammed the door to his small room in the back of the house, still screaming in

Romanian at the top of his lungs. Ilana begged us to leave, but I explained that I had come a long way and had a job to do for her relative. Stosh translated what Ilana said next: "Stephen is troubled by things we as mortals cannot explain." She went on to say that if the boy in the United States had similar problems, I was in great danger if I continued my investigation.

I wasn't about to turn tail and run for a number of reasons, the least of which was that now my curiosity had been raised a thousandfold! It was no longer a mission for the Sighisouras alone; the adventure now had the makings of a very intriguing paranormal or occult case for me. That the two boys were nearly the same age and seemingly exact duplicates added an eerie dimension to the "curse" theory. It was becoming clear to me that Charles and Stephen were linked by an ancient and malevolent bond. I was determined to find out how that link had been forged.

I begged Ilana to calm down and said that I would leave now if I could return again to speak with her and Stephen. Stosh translated for her that we could meet at a local tourist attraction where the caretaker was an expert on folktales and matters of the occult. Of course, I agreed, though I was both stunned and amused that the meeting was to take place in the Carpathian Mountains at none other than the Castle Dracula Hotel!

It was snowing lightly the following day when I arrived at the hotel. Aside from the signage, the "castle" looked like any normal midrange European hotel standing against the bleak gray sky. It was a typically older building, with small rooms and a tiny lobby, and was very cold. The lobby area did have a small showcase hawking Transylvanian wine—but the hotel was out of stock. The "kitschiness" of the surroundings was somewhat comforting as I thought about the seriousness of Charles's problem. Could he really be suffering from a vampire curse? I wondered. Aside from the outbursts and the clues Ilana had mentioned to me, I hadn't yet witnessed anything paranormal or unexplainable. I took that comfort with me as I checked into my room for a one night's stay. I was to meet with Ilana and her local "expert" that evening for dinner. It was around 4:30 P.M., so I thought I'd make good use of the time by consulting some of the books I had brought along that described various Romanian curse legends, particularly vampire myths and blood rituals. What rang clear through all of my reading was the link between young men and bloodletting, especially concerning soldiers and warriors. To drink the blood of an enemy was the ultimate victory and the key to everlasting life. These warrior myths, later mixed with Christian rituals of symbolically drinking the blood of Christ, had powerful psychological influences on young men in the region that in my mind could have created some bizarre psychic links between blood relations.

I theorized that either Stephen or Charles—whomever began the blood frenzy—was the main catalyst in the "curse."

Ilana arrived at 7:00 P.M. with her friend Christopher. We enjoyed a dinner consisting primarily of mixed meats and cabbage in the castle's modest dining room and then proceeded outside to be entertained by local dancers around a huge bonfire. The dance's origin was obviously rooted in hedonistic pagan beliefs. The elaborately costumed dancers dipped and swirled around the fire in a frenzied state and at times I thought they might actually leap into the flames. As we watched, transfixed by their gyrations, our gaze was interrupted by the band leader who handed out raw meat to be skewered and cooked over the fire. I learned that it was local custom to cook the meat over the fire and eat in celebration of simply being alive. I also heard whispers among the crowd that the meat was really to "fatten us up" and to make our blood "rich for the *nosferatu*."

I was eager to get out of the cold, and as we walked back to the castle, I took Christopher by the arm. As we walked, I made sure we were out of Ilana's earshot so I could bluntly ask him if he knew anything about vampire curses, especially involving links between family members. He nodded and said that despite modern disbelief, curses do exist. He explained that whether they are simply psychological manifestations brought on by some dysfunction or are of a paranormal origin, he had seen hundreds of instances of unexplained and sometimes terrifying occurrences. "My friend, to you this may seem startling, but to my people it is as common as any religious belief. Ilana told me of her son's problem and how you are investigating for the American cousins. I will tell you, the signs are all apparent. The boys are linked in their minds and there is a curse. They are vampires in their minds and the blood of the curse flows within them. It doesn't matter whether you believe that it is merely a neurosis or a supernatural phenomenon. No matter, there are certain rituals that must be performed to eliminate the curse. It is the only way the Sighisouras will have peace," Christopher said.

I had to take a breath. I expected some insight, but I never expected to hear my Romanian consultant nail the problem so matter-of-factly from the get-go.

We spoke for four hours that evening. Ilana and I learned that Charles and Stephen, because of their age and blood relation, were connected across the ocean in some telepathic conduit. One of the boys harbored the "curse" in his subconscious mind and was affecting his relative. Christian explained that regardless of the fact that the families had never physically met, the deep beliefs in the parents' minds and the recounting of the tales and stories associated with the curse had been deeply rooted in one of the boys' mind. After his entering manhood, the curse had taken hold. "It doesn't matter what we believe is possible. We simply do not understand how the mind, or the soul for that matter, really works. What matters is that the boys believe they are vampires, and they will act accordingly," Christopher told me.

Somehow, I reasoned, both families had planted the curse seed in their boys' minds, and in one of those minds the legend took hold. I could not explain how the minds connected across the Atlantic Ocean, other than by mere coincidence or perhaps some psychic connection that we have not yet discovered. But when we returned to Ilana's home and saw Stephen sitting at the kitchen table in front of a gutted rabbit, its entrails in his hands and his mouth and face drenched in blood, I knew that I had to contact the Sighisouras to see if Charles had gone this far as well. If he had, we needed to act immediately.

The Sighisouras were glad to hear from me. Before I could utter a word, Anna blurted out that Charles had done something terrible. "Calm down, calm down," I said to her. "Did it have to do with an animal?" I asked.

"Yes, yes. Charles was eating a freshly killed chicken in his room. It was horrible! There was blood everywhere. We think he is very ill," Anna said hysterically.

I said that I was close to solving the problem in Romania and that hopefully Charles would be okay. I told her that

Charles should see a doctor and a mental health professional in the interim, and she agreed. The truth was that Christopher had only mentioned that there was a possible solution, but we'd need to have Stephen's cooperation. What was required was that we conduct a psychodrama ritual that would convince Stephen that he was no longer cursed. The problem, according to Christopher, was that Stephen and Charles had to be *willing* to have the curse removed. "It is very appealing and sexy to be a vampire nowadays, or at least to think you are one. These boys may resist," Christopher said.

The Ritual

We were sure we would have a hard time convincing Stephen to participate in the ritual. We had even come up with a ruse that we thought would persuade him that he was performing an ancient rite of passage. But when we approached him, he said that he knew exactly what we were up to and that he'd gladly participate because it would only strengthen his abilities and insight into the "living death." "You may do as you please. I will gain strength from your attempts and my eyes will be completely opened to the immortality," Stephen said to us in his native tongue. His mother, distressed and crying, pleaded that we help her. "Please expel this evil from my son," she said. I couldn't help but think that this line sounded like it came from a late-night TV-movie script, but I was there and it was real.

Christopher and I entered an abandoned mausoleum on what he described as sacred ground about a quarter-mile from

Ilana's home. He said that the banishing ritual must be performed on consecrated earth primarily for the psychological influence it would have and partly because Christopher believed that it was essential to direct the powers—whatever they might be—to do our bidding and relieve the curse. We had to prepare dozens of bags of rare herbs including mugwort and mandrake root for incense burning, as well as pouring vials of absinthe, a potent drink used as a hallucinogenic for hundreds of years. Christopher explained that Stephen would have to release the curse from his subconscious and that the mind-altering substances would help. He also explained that the true catalyst that would break the curse was "fear." "We must remove the evil seduction by showing Stephen the horrors of the living death." I was prepared to conduct the unusual ritual until Christopher explained how we would expose the evil. I shook my head in disbelief when he said, "We must now prepare the corpse."

Christopher's aim was clearly to scare the hell out of Stephen by exposing him to a real dead body. Fortunately—or unfortunately for my sanity—the local Romanian laws governing the funeral business are much more lax than in the United States, so Christopher was able to procure a body through a close friend in the cemetery business. Christopher was serious about this ritual and he explained that although some theatrics were necessary, strange and unexplainable things often happened during the ceremonies.

Ilana, Stephen, and I took the short walk into the cemetery close to midnight the next day. Stephen was cocky and seemed eager to begin the ritual. His mother translated Stephen's comments that spoke of how this was his destiny and how he and his blood relations around the world would live forever and partake of the "pleasures of the night." If it wasn't for the despair on Ilana's face, I would have laughed at Stephen's vampire comic book dialogue. But the boy was serious. As we got closer to the mausoleum door, he became anxious and agitated, ripping his shirt open to expose his chest to the cold night air. We entered a candlelit stone room heavy with the smell of burning incense. Christopher stood at the far end. Only his face was visible from our vantage point, but I could make out a large wooden box on the ground before him. On top of the box was the bottle of green absinthe elixir and a large open book bound in torn leather that looked centuries old. Christopher wasted no time and asked Stephen in their native language if he was prepared to open his mind to the unknown and make the passage into manhood. Stephen walked directly toward Christopher, placed both of his palms on the box, and said, "I am a true vampire. Do what you will to me."

Stephen obeyed Christopher's instruction to drink the vial of absinthe. The mixed odors of the incense permeated the room and I felt myself becoming a bit light-headed. I knew it wouldn't be long until Stephen was swooning from the mixture of incense and absinthe. He began to sweat profusely as Christopher recited from the book. And then for about fifteen minutes Christopher conducted staccato questions and answers that I gathered were meant to challenge Stephen's belief in and allegiance to the supernatural. At first, Stephen was cocksure and arrogant, but as the smoke and absinthe kicked in, he began to sway and slur his speech.

Almost thirty minutes into the ritual, Christopher pushed Stephen back from the box, removed its lid, and exposed the corpse. Ilana gasped, but her son could do nothing but stand transfixed by the dead body below him. He could barely keep his footing as he turned repeatedly to look at his mother while Christopher's recitations became louder and faster. I learned later what Christopher was shouting repeatedly at the boy, "Do you relinquish your mortal soul to be immortal? Do you forsake all good for evil? Do you lust for the taste of blood? Do you seek the stench of death?"

Christopher pounded these words at Stephen time after time, finally standing directly in his face, spittle flying from his mouth and splashing the young boy's eyes. He grabbed Stephen by the shoulders and pushed his face into the box, only inches from the face of the corpse. "If you are to live as the dead, now live *with* the dead," Christopher screamed as he pushed Stephen into the box with the body. Stephen stumbled comically into the box landing face down, face to face with the corpse. Ilana screamed at Christopher that this was enough and to get her son out of the box, but Christopher held her arms against her chest and said it was necessary to break the curse. In all of the commotion, I wasn't sure myself if this was simply a scare tactic or if we were actually conjuring malevolent forces. The air in the crypt became dank and smelled of rotting flesh. The candles flickered wildly and we all began to sweat profusely. But Christopher showed the boy no mercy and asked for my assistance to hold him down into the box. "Don't let him up," he shouted at me, "until he tastes death."

The melee lasted nearly fifteen minutes, but it seemed as if we held the boy's body next to the corpse for more than an hour. Stephen finally spoke in a soft, calm voice saying that he had had enough and had witnessed true evil. Christopher translated his words: "Mother, I know now that mortal death is not to be feared. The *living* death is the soul's only torment."

Epilogue

During our journey back to the hotel I couldn't help but think that I had just witnessed an incredibly bizarre combination of psychodrama, homegrown psychotherapy, folk mythology, and "scared-straight" tactics. What was amazing was that it appeared to have worked and dispelled the "vampire blood curse" that had seduced Stephen's young mind. My sense of accomplishment was short lived when I remembered that this was only half the battle. I might have to perform the same ritual on the Sighisouras' son, Charles, back in Connecticut.

When I arrived at the hotel, the desk manager handed me a phone message. It was from the Sighisouras: "Mr. Johnson, we are happy to tell you that Charles miraculously has changed his attitude and habit within the last few hours." It went on to explain that the boy wept to his parents that he was wrong and sorry for his recent actions and that he loved them, and life, very much. I was happy to hear the good news. But I was stunned when I read the time the message was delivered: 2:00 A.M. Transylvania time . . . the *exact* time Stephen broke down during our cemetery ritual. The curse was broken not only in Romania but in a boy's bedroom halfway around the world.

4.

The Werewolf of Van Nuys

While I was sipping my coffee in Vincent's office, Silvana dropped some newspaper clippings on my desk. Although X-Investigations was officially affiliated with the private detective's company, our "office" consisted of a desk, a chair, a file cabinet, and a telephone. Vincent's rationale, which I fully understood, was that until the division became profitable we had to be mean and lean. And he also made sure that we didn't have any of our "kooky" ghost buster materials lying around where his regular clients might see them. So, out of habit I immediately picked up the clippings Silvana had dropped and was ready to toss them in my basket when a headline from a local southern California free-circulation paper grabbed my attention. It read, WEREWOLF PLAGUES LOCAL RESIDENTS. Even in our line of work, the word *werewolf* rarely pops up in our reading matter and I couldn't remember ever seeing a reference to werewolves in *any* newspaper, so I grabbed the clip and started reading about how the residents of an area in Van Nuys reported firsthand accounts of a half-man, half-animal creature that stalked the backyards of the

70

bedroom community, killing small animals and howling at the Moon!

Normally, we wouldn't take on an investigation unless we were solicited, but the more I read about this werewolf, the more intriguing the story became. What really piqued my curiosity was that the reporter on the local paper actually did his homework in the study of lycanthropy (from the Greek words *lukos* for wolf and *anthropos* for man—a field most people erroneously believe is the study of werewolves; however, it's a broader term that describes the interest in a psychological condition where people believe themselves to be animals of many kinds and sometimes adorn themselves with animal skins and teeth).

The reporter described how the locals told of a shape-shifting man in his thirties or forties who they at first see walking upright and then gradually bending at the waist until he appeared to be walking on all fours. The interesting part came from the reporter's accounts of how the eyewitnesses described a distinct canine odor that permeated the air whenever this half-man was spotted. The story also told of wet spots that appeared to be pools of drool that were found on the ground. Usual "big foot"–type spottings rarely mention anything but the visual sighting, and even then the accounts are far from accurate and in most cases vary from one person to another. But in this Van Nuys incident, over forty residents of the area were interviewed—some sought out and some volunteers—and they all described the werewolf in the exact same terms, mentioning the canine smells and pools of copious drool. The size of the man, the crouching, the bushiness of his hair, and even dead chickens and small pets that were mangled and torn were all corroborated by the reporter's sources.

It was just the kind of story that the mainstream newspapers would purposely ignore, thinking it was fabricated by a bunch of publicity seekers and would give a legitimate paper a bad name. And normally I myself would think it was nothing more than sensationalism. But when I asked Silvana for her opinion, she said something that started us off on one of the most unusual cases X-Investigations had ventured into. She said the story pointed out that most of the people who reported the "creature" were Mexican American—normally a very religious group and for them to embrace a werewolf mythos was very unusual. Silvana said, "These people are typically Roman Catholic and do not easily talk about strange occurrences. And almost all werewolf legends originated in northern Europe and had no Spanish influence. Any talk of half-man, half-animal creatures is extremely sacrilegious and is believed to be the devil's work. I believe, Robert, that if forty people were willing to speak of such a thing and risk sinning against God, then there must be something to the phenomenon. I am afraid that it is real."

Despite the fact that we had no contact in Van Nuys and we weren't being paid for our services, Silvana and I caught a plane to Los Angeles the next day. I felt that whatever we found in Van Nuys, whether it was a bona fide paranormal occurrence or not, we would gather useful background information for our files in the event we ever ran into such a case in the future. And as always in our investigations, we had a gut feeling that there was something strange happening in this middle-class American community. So strange that it had a number of residents acting like horror movie buffs. That was all we needed to justify our trip.

Silvana and I stayed at a Best Western near Interstate 405 in Van Nuys—about a mile from the newspaper's headquarters. We were expecting it to be typically bright and sunny in Los Angeles, but we hit town smack in the middle of the weather phenomenon called El Niño, which dumped days and days of rain on the otherwise pleasant environment. The locals were not accustomed to the gloom, and we were definitely not in the best of moods. It seemed fitting that we were investigating werewolves in this dark and dank setting. We wondered if perhaps the weather had somehow had an eerie causative effect on people typically accustomed to the bright and shiny California sun. But Jim Mitchell, the reporter for the *Valley Voice* who wrote the story, sounded cheery enough on the phone when I contacted him while we were still in New York to ask if he would be willing to guide us around in our investigation. Jim was more than happy to hear from us. He had taken a lot of heat for the story from his peers and was grateful that someone actually believed his work. So, after arriving at Los Angeles International, I wasted no time in calling the paper to set up an appointment with Jim.

When I asked for Jim, the newspaper receptionist said, "Oh, you want wolf boy." Mitchell was clearly getting it from all angles, so I immediately tried to make him feel that at least we were on his side. "Hi Jim, don't be bothered by those types—they're closed minded and they can't conceive of anything that exists outside of a *Terminator* movie," I said. I went on to explain that Silvana and I were eager to get moving on the case and wanted to speak to some of the witnesses. Silvana reminded me to ask if anyone had mentioned the full Moon aspect of the werewolf sightings. Jim said that no one had, which confirmed in Silvana's mind that this wasn't a gigantic hoax. "That would have been the first thing they would have said if this was a trick. It is so common and fits with the legend. It looks for real to me," Silvana said. But

I pointed out that the area was socked in with overcast skies and if it was a hoax they wouldn't be able to explain how they knew it was full Moon. "You don't have to *see* the Moon to know it is full, Robert. Just read the newspaper, look at a calendar, or go on the Internet," Silvana replied. I was again reminded why I needed a partner.

Eyewitnesses

We arranged to meet Jim at a local coffee shop to discuss the case before we met any of his star witnesses. He told us that there were two sisters who were the most vocal and articulate and who happened to have seen the alleged werewolf on more than one occasion. They lived about a quarter-mile apart, so their testimony allowed us to construct a geographic area that we could stake out. Jim explained that both of these women had seen the creature numerous times and had supplied the most graphic descriptions of its appearance. I asked if they seemed to be normal, everyday people and if there was anything about their behavior or background that would have made Jim think they might be just bored housewives looking for a different kind of gossip thrill. But Jim assured me that both Kari and Josie were as normal as could be and were upstanding citizens in their community with good jobs—Kari was a nurse and Josie a caterer—and there was no record of them ever participating in anything even remotely bizarre. That's when Silvana chimed in and asked if they were religious people. "All of the families in this Mexican community are religious—Catholics, most of them," Jim answered.

Silvana nodded to me and I recognized that look in her eyes that meant we were about to embark on a juicy case.

Jim called Kari from the coffee shop and asked when we could meet. She was concerned about who we were but Jim assured her that we wanted to get to the bottom of the strange goings-on, so she agreed. It was about 7:00 P.M. on a Friday, and Kari told Jim that we could come over right away.

As we drove down the street to Kari's house, we could have been on any suburban American block. All of the houses were standard California ranch style with large front lawns and two-car garages. Everything seemed normal except for the distinct absence of playing children and barking dogs. It was oddly quiet—too quiet. When we arrived at Kari's yellow-and-white home at the end of the cul de sac, she was already at the front door waving hello. After we made our formal introductions, I politely asked, "Kari, I noticed that there is no barking on this street. In fact I haven't seen one pet, or children playing outdoors for that matter."

She looked at Jim and told me that since the sightings of the werewolf man, children and pets were kept indoors after dusk. "Some small pets have disappeared and a neighbor who raises chickens, which is not uncommon for our people, has had many killed. We are taking no chances," Kari said.

I asked Kari to describe in detail what she had seen and when she first saw the werewolf of Van Nuys. "I was bringing my children home from open school night about six weeks ago. It was just about the time El Niño started, so it was very foggy and damp. My son, Jorge, asked if we could go to the local soccer field before we came home to find a ball he had left there earlier that day. He said he didn't think anyone would have taken it because he kicked it in some bushes under the trees at the edge of the park. So I agreed to go with him and we walked into the small forest area to find his ball. Just as Jorge was picking up his ball, I heard some rustling in the bushes nearby. At first, I thought it was a cat or maybe a squirrel or possum. But it looked very large and made a lot of noise. I became frightened and grabbed Jorge's hand and started to run. But my curiosity got the better of me, and I had to look back at what now appeared to be a big hairy back of an animal that was crouched over. I had never seen anything that large. At first, I thought it was a bear. I couldn't help myself and I let out a gasp. That's when it happened."

"What happened?" Silvana and I asked in unison.

"When I gasped, the thing raised up on two legs—like a man but covered in hair—it turned its head to look at me." Kari had to stop to compose herself. But I pressed her to continue. "The face was not a man's. It had yellow eyes and it was drooling. It looked like the face of a German shepherd dog. But I believe it was a wolf!"

My first impulse was to ask Kari how she could have possibly thought she saw a man with a wolf's body and face, but I opted instead to ask if she wasn't sure that maybe someone was playing a trick on people by running around in a werewolf costume. She said that she knew the difference and the terror had a lot more to do with the entire scenario and not just the creature's appearance. She mentioned the odor—like wet dog—and the growling, guttural noise that came from the creature's mouth. "These were not sounds that could have been made by a man. I grew up with many animals and I know the difference between a human sound and an animal's," Kari said. "It is also the hair that we found caught on the bushes when we returned the next day. It was very coarse—like a dog's."

I asked if the hair had been analyzed. Kari said it hadn't but that she had saved a clump. I immediately instructed Silvana to locate a lab and get us some results. I asked Jim why he hadn't followed up himself—since positive results would have added credence to his story. He told me that at the time Kari wouldn't part with it. Now she said, "I can only give it to someone whom I feel really believes in what we saw that night. There are many strange things that happen in the world and the unbelievers will only think I am crazy. I feel you know about things that can't be explained."

As we drove away from Kari's house, I thought that this was turning out to be an interesting investigation. I couldn't recall the last time I read, or even heard, about a werewolf sighting or a case of psychological lycanthropy, no less one that was reported by dozens of people. I was anxious to get the results of the hair analysis, so we dropped Silvana off at a lab that Jim recommended in downtown L.A. and drove on to interview another key witness to the sighting, a professor at the Northridge campus of California State University. Sam Glazik, a natural sciences instructor, was the most down-to-earth person imaginable. I was immediately struck by his articulate and sophisticated manner after Jim introduced us. I knew that if anyone we interviewed would be skeptical and able to give us an unbiased and factual account of what he saw, it would be Sam. In fact, the first thing he said to me was that he was glad to meet us but that he really didn't believe in the paranormal or the occult and he hoped we could find a logical explanation for his account. "My wife thinks I'm drinking at night after my classes. But I know what I saw, and it *is* strange indeed," he said.

It seemed odd that in the midst of the vibrant college campus we were all talking about the possibility of a wild man-beast running around a metropolitan area, but that's one incident that makes X-Investigations the fascinating entity it is. We handle the "kooky," the absurd, the far out, and the unbelievable cases that almost no "regular" authority would touch. Unless there's a murder or report of abuse, the police and even bona fide academics will not pursue the strange and unexplained. Aside from using some psychics in police murder cases, employing the paranormal is considered "nutty" and a waste of time. But there are thousands of unsolved police cases that are currently open without explanation. Silvana and I both knew when we began our venture that we would be perceived as the stuff of TV and movies. But we also knew that we had an instinctive, inherent need and drive—a "calling" that allowed us to put logic aside and open our minds to what seems to be impossible. We had both done this from an early age and it has opened our eyes. Once they are opened, they can never be closed. I recognized that Sam's eyes were now open and he didn't know how to deal with it. It was our job to welcome him aboard.

"First off, professor, you'll be happy to know that there have been a number of witnesses who not only saw what you saw, but have actual hard evidence to back it up. We're analyzing a clump of hair right now that could set the stage for this entire investigation," I said. Sam smiled and said that made him feel a little better, and then he told us his story. He had been leaving his last class one evening about 10:00 P.M. He had had to park fairly far from the building where the class was held because he had arrived late in the day. The pathway to the car lot cut through an open field and then through a patch of trees and temporary steel picnic tables. As Sam headed toward the lot, he saw someone running in the distance about two hundred yards in front of him. He thought at first it was someone chasing after his dog because he heard a low growling and barking sound. As the shadowed figure moved closer, Sam said it looked as if it was running bent at the waist. He thought maybe the man held a dog's leash and that was what was causing him to bend. But as he got closer—about twenty-five yards away—the creature streaked from side to side in and out of the trees, and Sam was shocked to see that it was very hairy and its head was quite pointed. "It was its face that really spooked me. I thought it was some kind of motorcycle helmet at first because the front of his head had an elongated nose. Sometimes these helmets have that shape. But then I noticed the flowing hair, not only on the head but on the body as well, so I knew it wasn't a helmet at all. It was the thing's head, and as I got closer I was transfixed. It saw me, stopped, and stared right at me. I was really freaked out when it looked straight at me," Sam said.

What disturbed Sam most was the creature's eyes. He described them as bright yellow orbs that shone like two solid-color marbles. "I knew this was no man when I saw the eyes. And if it was a Halloween mask it was a damn good one. But why would a prankster be darting in and out of trees. He would be somewhere he could frighten people. Oh, I was frightened all right, but he wasn't laying in wait for me. But I discovered why he was there after he ran away and I saw the dead squirrels mangled on the ground. This thing was eating dinner," Sam told us.

I asked Sam if he had any hard evidence like Kari's to back up his story, but he told me the only thing left at the scene were the dead squirrels and he surely wasn't going to save their carcasses. But he did add that although no one would come forward, there were other people at his school who admitted to him that they also saw some strange type of

man-beast wandering after hours in the vicinity of the parking
lot. They referred to him as the "homeless guy," to avert
alarming the school's population, but from what I could gather
they were protecting themselves from being labeled crackpots.

After our meeting with Sam, I called Silvana and told her
to meet us back at the motel. We managed to use the hotel's
conference room to discuss the case. What I wanted to do was
draw a map of the local area and with Jim's help pinpoint all
of the spots the werewolf had been sighted. I knew from the
newspaper accounts that all of the sightings occurred within
about a three-mile radius, but I wanted to see if I could discover a pattern based on time, days of the week, and, of
course, the full Moon. We needed to also gather the exact
accounts of the other witnesses and draw conclusions based
on their sightings and particular "clues." Most people simply
saw the strange-looking creature darting about or running
with something in its mouth.

We also had reports of growling and howling. A man who
lived close to Kari mentioned that he walks his dog around
1:00 A.M. each night and occasionally he heard howling that
was very different from a dog's. "I know a dog's howls, and
there are a number of coyotes up in the hills that sometimes
come down, especially when it's real hot and dry. But one
night I heard this howl that was much different. And, it was
very close. At first I thought it was someone's TV, but it was
too real. This was only a few blocks from my house. Then the
next morning my neighbor tells me some wild dogs killed his
chickens. It was no dog that killed them chickens. Not that
night," the old man said.

We finally got the lab results about the hair, and although
I wasn't shocked at the findings I was surprised to learn that

the hair was canine, but inconclusive. It could have come from a dog or a wolf. And even if it did come from a wolf's coat, a person so inclined could have made a costume containing the hair. But whether what we were after was a real werewolf, a psychotic, or a prankster, we now knew that someone or some *thing* was involved with the occult or knew enough about it to perpetrate a werewolf sighting. If animals were indeed victims, then who knew if humans would be next? What we needed to find out was how we could lure the werewolf and corner it to confirm what it really was. The patterns we saw indicated that it made appearances only in the evening and interestingly enough during a waxing Moon cycle (the time building to the full Moon). There were no sightings during a waning Moon cycle.

During the next two weeks, Silvana and I scoured the area where the sightings were reported, looking for clues. Unfortunately, because this was such a heavily trafficked area that had regular maintenance either by homeowners or the local municipality, we found very few traces of what could have been our creature. One particular area that had more than one sighting and was not far from a local Santería botanica kept recurring to me as one that we might want to further investigate. It was a curious shop because it carried a variety of occult products, and not just the traditional botanica supplies. I noticed a number of Wiccan items in the store window and a fully stocked herb and potion counter. We decided that we would concentrate on this area near the store for seven consecutive nights during the next waxing Moon period.

Jim helped us hire a nondescript van (we felt like CIA operatives) and loaded it with supplies from the Spy Shop in L.A. We packed in video recording equipment with night recording features, sound equipment that could pick up whispers a hundred yards away, digital cameras, and some of our home-made devices for gathering samples. Jim's brother, a local sheriff's deputy, even managed to get us an animal tranquilizer gun, just in case we were attacked by whatever lurked in the streets of Van Nuys.

The Wolf Trap

Three nights had passed with no sighting. The three of us rotated sleeping and keeping watch on the area. The most interesting thing we had seen so far was an ordinary howling-and-screaming alley cat fight. Silvana told us that a "fight of cats" always precedes some traumatic event in her native country's folklore. (I remember a cat fight always preceded someone's shoe being thrown at them in Brooklyn where I grew up.) Jim and Silvana were getting antsy and suggested that we move to another spot—one closer to a wooded area that fit better with the werewolf's profile. But I had a reason to stick it out, one that proved to be correct.

On the fourth evening, at about 10:30, Silvana's cell phone rang. The call was from a close friend of Kari's who had gotten our number in case she had ever spotted anything strange. The locals stuck together, especially when it came to protecting their families. I could see Silvana's eyes widen even in the dimly lit van. "We must go to Krebs Street. The creature has been seen. Do you know where this is, Jim?" Jim knew the block and we both asked Silvana simultaneously what had happened. "A little girl in her room. The werewolf was there," was all Silvana could reply. "We must go now!"

When we arrived at the house on Krebs Street, the police were just leaving. As we approached the front door, a large man in a white T-shirt with the legend VALLEY CONCRETE in red letters blocked our path and asked who we were and what we wanted. Jim identified himself as a reporter, which immediately put the giant on the defensive. We learned that the man was the girl's father from her mother, Felicia, who came out and explained to him that we were the investigators searching for the beast. She welcomed us in and began her harrowing tale.

Felicia told us that she put her eight-year-old daughter, Theresa, to bed as she did every night at about 7 o'clock. Theresa slept in the back room on the first floor. The parents were in the living room watching TV when they heard a snarling noise from their backyard. Little did they know that Theresa was awake sitting up in bed looking at the "big dog" trying to push its way into her room. Felicia said, "We always leave the window cracked for air, but it has a screen and a lock so it can only open so far. Theresa was sleeping when she heard a noise like scratching against the screen. My little girl told me she sat up in bed in the dark and saw a dog with two large yellow eyes pushing its nose against the screen and using its head to push up the window. That's when we heard the growling and we ran into her room."

When the parents entered the room, Theresa's eyes were fixed on the window, but the werewolf had disappeared from sight. We asked if we could enter the room and Felica obliged us. The first thing we noticed was a wet spot that covered about a six-inch radius on the screen. I asked Felicia if it had been touched and she said that she had cleaned it off with a household cleaner. I was hoping we could have gotten a sample for our analysis.

We searched the area outside of the window and it was just our luck that it began to rain. As we were rummaging around, we heard movement in the bushes that bordered the side of the house. I tried to grab Silvana's arm, but she was too quick and ran directly toward the noise with her digital camera in hand. I lost my footing in the mud and by the time I regained my composure Silvana was already near the source of the noise. I heard a growling sound and more rustling. Silvana shouted, "I think it's here, Robert!" When I got to the spot, Silvana had already shot dozens of frames, and although we all stomped through the bushes in search of the werewolf, we couldn't find anything. I had a hunch so I told the crew to jump back into the van and return to our stakeout spot by the botanica. I told Silvana to check the shots on the digital camera as we drove away. Out of almost thirty pictures, there was only one that showed what appeared to be a man hunched over and running through the bushy area. We could definitely make out a figure and flowing hair, and we were encouraged by our first real break.

I was now confident that we were on the right track. But Silvana asked me why we were headed back to the stakeout spot when we had just seen evidence that the creature was some distance away. I explained that I noticed that the botanica had carried a variety of herbs used in occult ritual and workings, including nightshade and henbane, plants that contain psychoactive alkaloids. These substances, when used as a rubbing salve or ingested as a tonic, cause hallucinatory effects that have been recorded in a number of instances of lycanthropy. "Occult lore tells of many stories where those who wish to shape change into animals—especially wolves—ingest these herbal ingredients to act out their wishes," I said.

"My hunch is that our werewolf has been rummaging through the botanica's dumpster in search of these ingredients. From what I understood, the effects last only a short time, so if our werewolf is hooked he'll be back for more in a short time."

We were disappointed that our monster didn't show that night. We all fell asleep in the van and were awoken by the clang of the front gate of the botanica opening for the day. I decided to walk over and speak with the woman unlocking the door. She was understandably anxious about an unshaven man in rumpled clothes asking questions about werewolves at 10:00 A.M. But after I explained who I was and what X-Investigations was all about, Maria, the owner, was friendly and cooperative. Over a cup of freshly brewed coffee, I explained our case and she nodded that she had heard the rumors. "Some people have come to me asking advice, but I tell them I do not fool around in the spirit world," Mary said. She didn't offer any hard clues and she couldn't tell me of anyone who regularly asked for nightshade or henbane. She did caution that these ingredients are sometimes poisonous and that we should be careful with them. I assured her they weren't for us but asked her how she disposed of her old herbs. She said she tossed them in the Dumpster outside in green bags because they are biodegradable. She would do this every so often whether or not the stock was old, just to be sure she sold only the freshest products. It dawned on me, that if our werewolf was looking for the hallucinogens, he had to get there before the trash was picked up. We were seeking him at night when he was prowling. What we needed to do was nab him in the day.

I asked Maria if anyone regularly went through her trash and she said that there was an old homeless man from the woods who would come down and had to be chased away.

Coincidentally, he was interested in the green trash bags more than any other. Maria described him as a tall man with a hunched-over walk and very long hair. "He comes down from the hills. I think he lives up there in the caves. He has many animals with him," Maria said.

Epilogue

When "Old Sam," the homeless mountain man, was taken into custody by the sheriff's department, he was questioned about his whereabouts and actions and what he was taking from the Dumpster near Mary's store. Jim was able to get some inside information from a friend of his at the sheriff's department who said that the shrinks who examined Sam had determined that he suffered from psychotic episodes and had multiple personality disorders. He noted that Sam had a number of animal hides and skins that could be worn like ceremonial clothing. A common werewolf legend tells of would-be werewolves who made belts from wolf hides that they'd wear as they were shape changing. This could have explained the hair clump Kari had found near her sighting.

Sam was committed to a state mental facility for observation, but despite the fact that we had spent a very long time on this "no pay" case, we decided to remain in the Van Nuys area for another week. Since there were no further reports of werewolf sightings and we had run out of time, we were fairly satisfied that Sam was either a deranged person with some occult leanings or that our real werewolf had gotten away.

We landed at John F. Kennedy International Airport the next day. As soon as I turned on my cell phone, I got a message beep to call Jim in L.A. I barely said hello when Jim said, "Robert, there's been another werewolf sighting." I chuckled as I asked him if Old Sam was back on the street. But Jim said that he checked with his buddy at the sheriff's department who told him Sam had been committed permanently. He sounded very concerned and added, "Here's another thing, Rob. My buddy got me a copy of the transcript of Sam's talks with the shrinks. This is the last thing he said to his doctor. Are you ready for this?" I said "Shoot," and Jim read me these lines from the transcript:

DOCTOR: So, Sam, you understand that you are not really an animal at all, but are a sound human, correct?

SAM: Oh, I understand, doctor. But you must understand also. There are many, many, more of my kind out there. And we are very, very hungry.

5.

The Satanists Next Door

My old friend Aggie, a chain-smoking, middle-aged, third-generation Irishwoman, has lived in Hell's Kitchen on the Upper West Side of Manhattan all of her life. She had seen Hell's Kitchen change from a predominantly Irish working-class section of New York City to a black and Hispanic neighborhood and then gentrify into a new yuppie haven. Aggie's home was never what you would call tranquil. In her youth, she'd had to be wary of gang violence and street toughs, and the changes over the years brought new and different kinds of criminal activity. Despite it all, Aggie survived and was never really very frightened about anything in her neighborhood. Her attitude was always that as long as she could walk and talk and had the Lord at her back, she was okay. But then she discovered that Satanists lived in her apartment building.

Aggie was the superintendent of an eight-story walk-up tenement building located in the Fifties on Eleventh Avenue. The neighborhood was experiencing quite a change in the late 1990s as apartments all over New York were becoming more and more expensive. It was the typical Manhattan scenario:

the best neighborhoods become pricey, young people can't afford them, so the boundaries expand into poorer and under-developed areas. This was happening quickly in Hell's Kitchen, which is now called Clinton.

I knew Aggie since I was a child. She and my aunt Carol were the best of friends, and since Carol passed away Aggie had kept in touch with me. She and my aunt were devout Roman Catholics and they always feared that my interest in the occult was putting my life and immortal soul in danger. They needed regular assurance that I was fine and wasn't becoming possessed or going over to the "other side." In fact, Aunt Carol would never actually pronounce the word *devil*. Whenever she referred to him, she would say "divil," with an *i* in place of the *e*, explaining that she wouldn't give him the benefit of calling him by his proper name. Her bit of Irish wisdom explained it this way, "Well, how do you call some-one when you want them? You say their name. If you never say their name, they'll never answer you. So you don't want the Dark One answering you now do you?"

So when Aggie called me at home one Saturday morning to see how I was doing, I wasn't surprised to hear from her. But I did notice a faint sound of concern in her voice. I asked if anything was troubling her. She told me that I might have thought she was going loony in her old age, but she recently heard that the couple in apartment 7S was a bit strange. I asked Aggie what she meant by "strange," and after a few minutes of hemming and hawing she spit it out. "Oh, Bobby, the people are divil worshipers! They pray to the Dark One. To Satan himself," she said hysterically. After a few minutes of trying to calm her down, I figured out what she was trying to tell me. Apparently, new tenants in the building who rented the apartment next to the long-time tenants in apartment 7S were asking other people in the building if they knew the couple next door to them. They said they were concerned because they heard noises and music playing. At times, they heard a gong being struck and there were all sorts of "weird" people, many dressed in black, coming in and out of the apartment.

I told Aggie that this could be nothing more than crazy rumor, particularly because the people in 7S had lived there for more years than Aggie herself, and that she should dismiss it as nonsense. At first, Aggie agreed to let it go and not to worry. But as we were ending our conversation, she said that she just might ask her parish priest to make a visit on 7S "just to be on the safe side." Considering the litigious society we now live in, I told Aggie that wasn't a good idea and she should really mind her own business. "But, Bobby, I can't mind my business. If these people are black-hearted divil worshipers, they will infect the whole building. Who knows what blasphemies they've been committing up there? I'm the super of the building. The good Lord will never forgive me if I just close my eyes to evil. I never done it in the past and I ain't about to do it now, my boy."

It's hard to argue with a feisty old Irish dame, so I appeased her by asking to hold off on calling the parish priest and let me see what I could do. Aggie thanked me profusely and reminded me that Aunt Carol was smiling in heaven at that very moment. It was comforting to picture my aunt happy and at peace. So the Irish charm worked, and my next case for X-Investigations began. I was about to discover if there were truly diabolical events going on in apartment 7S in the middle of Manhattan. But my real concern was to keep Aggie safe both physically and mentally.

The Rituals

The first thing I needed to do was brush up on *real* satanic ritual, not the mumbo jumbo that we're bombarded with in newspapers and TV. After spending many years studying the occult, the one thing I am certain about is that most common knowledge about almost any discipline, sect, lodge, or religion is usually wrong. Occult topics make for juicy sensationalist headlines and sound bites and they're exploited at the expense of people who take their beliefs seriously. It's easy to take a shot ay anything strange or out of the ordinary because the people who practice esoteric disciplines don't fight back, often out of fear of being labeled kooks and weirdoes.

Interestingly enough, the single most illuminating fact I discovered about modern Satanism is that there has never been one case of ritual sacrifice, abduction, mutilation, or death linked to *any* satanic organization or individual, despite the hysterical claims of the media and religious fundamentalists. And this comes straight from the FBI and other government law enforcement agencies. Oh yes, there are tons of historical data about heinous crimes perpetrated by those who claim to be Satanists, but there is no hard evidence for any of it. Of course, I discovered voluminous tomes describing arcane rituals and "sell-your-soul" pacts with the devil that ranged from silly to downright hair raising. And there are dozens of "documented" cases of demonic possession and the obligatory exorcism to go along with them. But I never experienced any real possession in any case I've conducted and I always find it suspect that the exorcism craze started shortly after William Peter Blatty's book and the movie *The Exorcist* that was published in the 1970s. So I really needed to know what was disturbing Aggie so much in order to conduct a legitimate investigation. If she had Satanists in her building and they were indeed conjuring demons or conducting some real evil, I wanted proof.

I met with Aggie later that week and asked her to explain just what her problem was with the people in 7S besides the odd people coming in and out. I took a hard line with her, despite the fact that I cared about Aggie as much as I did my own aunt. I knew Aggie was prone to gossip and exaggeration, so specifics were vital to this case. After a few sips of tea (with a special added ingredient of cheer to loosen the tongue), Aggie began explaining the circumstances in 7S. "It first started with the smells, Bobby. You know I clean the halls almost every day—when my back allows me to—and there was this one day that I smelled quite a peculiar odor coming from the apartment. It was a smell I never noticed before, some kind of burning incense, but not the pretty kind that smells like violets or strawberry. No, this was a smell like burning cork or an old tree being burned. And it had a sweet odor about it, too. A mix of strange smells that reminded me of them Indian restaurants, but stronger. So strong it was burning my eyes and nose. And I'm used to the ammonia, so it takes a lot to burn my senses," Aggie said.

I listened but said to her that people burn incense all the time and it's nothing to be alarmed about. It didn't seem strange to me at all until Aggie mentioned that the incense was now burning twenty-four hours a day and permeating the entire floor for days at a time. She told me that the burning would begin in the evening and then people would arrive—most of them dressed in black and some looking like they didn't even belong in this era. I asked if they were wearing costumes but Aggie said no, they were wearing period clothing mostly from the 1940s and 1950s—men in hats, women with nylon stockings and polka-dot dresses, and even a fellow in a zoot suit. Not what one would call traditional "satanic" garb for sure. (I was expecting to hear of people coming to the apartment dressed in ceremonial wizard's cloaks and hooded monk's capes, not zoot suits.) As the details of the case got stranger, I began to seriously wonder if dear Aggie might have been sniffing the ammonia for one too many years.

She went on to talk about the odd noises and the chanting that followed what she was now calling the "ceremony." This was Aggie's description:

Once all of the people arrived—sometimes ten or twenty of them—the smells would get stronger and stronger. I heard a lot of laughing and talking just like a regular party was going on. There'd be men talking loudly and women giggling and there was music. But not the kind of music that you'd expect young people to be playing (even though I hate that rap and rock 'n' roll stuff), it was classical kind of stuff like Beethoven and Mozart but not regular tunes that you'd recognize. These were very somber like, gloomy music with heavy beats like funeral marches. The music would start around nine o'clock and continue all night.

Sometimes the classical music changed into organ music, like what you might hear in a church or in a theater that had the *Phantom of the Opera* in it.

It would happen like this once a month usually . . . but never on the same days. Sometimes it was on a weekday and sometimes it was on the weekend. But that was the "normal" stuff. It was around midnight when things got spooky. I stayed up late the second time I heard the weird get-together going on. And I was just about to go to bed when I heard the gong. Just like a Chinese gong, it sounded three times and things got real quiet in 7S. Then in about a few minutes I heard a man talking, reciting like he was reciting passages from a Bible or something. Then I heard the gong again and it was struck another three times. Now when the man recited I heard the whole group say the same things he was saying . . . real strange words like *"Belial,"* and *"Toth"* and words I did understand like *"flesh"* and *"darkness"* and even the word *"hell"*! I didn't much understand what they were doing that first time I heard the crazy goings-on, but when they all let out in one loud voice, *"Hail, Satan!"* *I nearly fell out of my bed!!*

I had to admit that Aggie's account of what went on in the apartment was intriguing. And if it had happened on only one occasion, I would have dismissed it as being a prank or some kind of play rehearsal or something with a logical explanation. But Aggie and a number of the other tenants in the building had heard what sounded very much to me like a ritual of some sort. That fact, coupled with the odd incense burning, began to rouse my curiosity and I felt there might actually be something to the 7S phenomenon. I thought this was enough to warrant an investigation and I was satisfied that I had enough to go on to start building data for X-Investigations' case files. But little did I know that this was just the beginning. What Aggie described next definitely fit into the realm of the paranormal.

Sadie's Curse

I was with Aggie for at least six hours discussing the odd goings-on in her building. She was very forthcoming, describing what she had heard, what the neighbors were saying, and the strange odors that emanated from the apartment. She even explained how the couple, whom I later learned were Caroline and Arthur Hastings—originally from London—had recently gotten a new pet dog after their old dog expired suddenly. The old dog, a large black rottweiler, was seldom seen outside of the apartment and many of the "curious" tenants wondered when the animal was ever walked to relieve itself. "We just kinda assumed that the dog was walked late at night when everyone was asleep," Aggie said.

The new dog, a large black chow, on the contrary, was seen quite often, usually just before midnight. I was amazed that so many people in the building had the time or the inclination to pay attention to their odd neighbors' habits in such detail. They had become a tenement building spy network that regularly reported their findings to each other over afternoon tea and cookies. This made me believe that some bored tenants needed a little spice in their lives and what I was hearing was grossly exaggerated. But the vivid descriptions that were told by Sadie, Aggie's friend, and her subsequent "curse" kept me on the case.

Sadie and I met in Aggie's apartment on a Thursday afternoon. The plumbing in the place, if not the original pipes, had to be at least fifty years old. The sink was a large green basin with the main pipe exposed underneath. The hot and cold water pipes leading to the faucets could be seen running along the wall and into the ceiling. I was startled when Aggie turned on the water and the air pressure caused a loud rhythmic banging before the water spouted out. I said to Aggie that she should worry about her plumbing being possessed by demons, and not one of her apartments. She chuckled politely but immediately turned the conversation over to Sadie, which was a little disturbing to me because Aggie was always one to follow up on a good jibe and would give it right back to me. She asked Sadie, another middle-aged woman who had lived in the building for years, to tell me what had happened to her. Sadie said she thought I would think she was nuts, but I assured her that I heard many unusual stories and the last thing I would think at this point was that she was crazy, considering all of the trouble Aggie had gone through to get me involved.

Sadie lived on the eighth floor of the building, and one evening as she was going downstairs to throw away her trash she passed 7S. It just so happened that some black-clad young people were entering the apartment at the same time. Sadie told me she was staring at the group because of all of the mystery surrounding the apartment when suddenly one baldheaded young man with a prominent tattoo that looked like a serpent's tail jutting out from under the collar of his shirt and up his neck, looked Sadie straight in the eye. He dropped his gaze to the Star of David that she wore around her neck and said, "What are you staring at, old woman? Do we frighten you? You think we're freaks who worship Satan or something? Well, that trinket around your neck's not going to protect you. In fact, I spit on your impotent God and I curse your stupid religion *and* you."

Needless to say, Sadie was shaken up by the encounter and hurried away to complete her errand. It took her nearly fifteen minutes to calm down and regain her composure, and she told me she was in no hurry to pass the apartment again until every one of the guests was out of sight. Once back in her own apartment, Sadie felt safe and went to bed around 11:00 P.M. But the surly man's words kept ringing in her head, especially the part about her being cursed. "I never believed in curses, but I admit that what he said bothered me and made me toss and turn that night. It was the way that bald man said it to me—so full of hate—and that tattoo on his neck frightened me. I will tell you that I did have a strange dream that made me feel as though I was choking and I awoke around 3:00 A.M., startled and thinking about the earlier incident. And that's when the weird things began."

Sadie got up to go to the bathroom and noticed a large black spot in the corner of her bathroom floor. It was difficult for her to see what caused the spot with only her night-light illuminating the path to the bathroom. As Sadie got closer, she bent down and removed her glasses to get a better look. The black spot was not simply a large mark on the floor, but rather, it was glistening. At least that's what Sadie thought at first. As she leaned closer, she realized that the spot was not a spot at all but a large pool of black insects—water bugs— that were huddled together, undulating in the corner and attempting to climb their way up the corner of the bathroom wall. She screamed and slammed the bathroom door shut.

She said she could actually hear the bugs clicking on the tiles in a disgusting frenzy. Sadie ran back into her bedroom and jumped under the bedcovers for safety. She was hoping that she was just dreaming and that there were no bugs crawling around the floor, but the clicking noises became louder and louder, almost deafening. She told me that just when she thought she couldn't take it anymore, the noises stopped. She waited for about ten minutes until she had the courage to return to the bathroom to see if the water bugs were still there. She was about to get out of bed but realized that every time she removed the covers from her body, she found herself covered again. "I would pull down the blanket and try to get out of bed, but the covers were on me again! I did this many, many times and I was very frightened. It was like I was experiencing the same scene over and over again and I couldn't escape," Sadie said.

Once Sadie realized she wasn't dreaming, she panicked, screaming and flailing her arms so violently she finally escaped from the bedcovers. Despite the early hour, she immediately called Aggie, sobbing on the phone as she tried to explain what was happening in her apartment.

Aggie threw on a robe and went to Sadie's aid. As Sadie told Aggie her story, her eyes darted repeatedly to the closed bathroom door. Aggie wanted to see the phenomenon for herself and opened the bathroom door, only to discover that there was nothing but a wet spot where Sadie said there had been hundreds of water bugs scrambling and climbing up the wall. "It was the damnedest thing, Bobby," Sadie told me. "I know what I saw, but when Aggie opened that door there was nothing . . . not a bug in sight." Of course, I explained to Sadie that her imagination may have gotten the better of her what with the dream and the upsetting encounter earlier in the evening, but then she reached into her housedress pocket and pulled out a Polaroid photo of her bathroom floor teeming with water bugs in the very spot Sadie had claimed they were gathered. "I took this picture the very next night because I knew I wasn't going crazy. These Satanists were having some kind of loud ceremony or orgy down there that I heard through the walls. They woke me up, but I was prepared. They put a curse on me and here's the proof," Sadie said as she handed me the picture.

It was hard to explain for sure, but Sadie did have a photo to back up her story. Further investigations into the building turned up other bizarre events. A few of the tenants noted that the black chow's eyes changed color from black to green. They swore to me that they saw the dog a number of times late at night and its eyes were never the same. They said that they knew it was the same dog each time because it had an identifying grey spot near its left ear. Aggie was convinced the dog was a demon that took the shape of an animal and that's why its eye color changed. "It's a demon dog from hell that does the bidding of those creeps," she said.

Other reports told of strong odors, slamming doors in the hallways, insect sightings, and an overall sense of dread. A young couple on the ground floor told me that each Sunday after they attended the local Roman Catholic church they would always feel a sense of calm after they left and returned home, but in the last few months they felt fine until they entered their building. "Recently, that sense of peace was suddenly washed away as soon as we got home. Sometimes, we would get into arguments over nothing. It's eerie, disturbing," the couple said. The neighbors who lived next to 7S in apartment 7R, who originally started the inquiries because of the strange noises they heard, confirmed the odd aura of the building on Eleventh Avenue. They said they were experiencing a string of bad luck unlike they'd ever had before.

I couldn't dismiss all of the claims made by the tenants, nor could I believe everything I was being told. What I did know was that my initial curiosity had turned into a two-week investigation and I had to get to the bottom of the problem. At a tenant meeting organized by Aggie, I heard clamors and demands for exorcisms and cleansing spells. Sadie said we needed to have the parish priest bless the building immediately. The couple next door to 7S wanted the Hastingses evicted! But I convinced them to let me experience firsthand one of the "meetings" in 7S that they claimed sparked the weird events. I asked Aggie to call me the next time the group gathered and I would tell them what I thought they should do. Her call came two nights later.

The Satanists Celebrate

"It's happening, Bobby. The Satanists are gathering tonight. I already heard the furniture being moved and that's always the beginning. They have to make room for their orgies and black masses, "Aggie said. It was about 6:30 Friday night, and I told her to calm down and that I would be there before 8. We had set up a makeshift spy center in a utility closet down the hall from 7S, where I could secretly observe and record what was happening. I had some electronic gear—a supersensitive listening and eavesdropping device with an attached recorder; a pinhole camera with a fiber-optic cable that we mounted on the top molding of the Hastingses' front door; and a hand-held digital video camera with extreme low-light sensitivity. It was advantageous to be working with a licensed private investigator for the James Bond gadgets alone. Because Aggie was the superintendent of the building, we knew that although what we were doing was technically an invasion of privacy, loopholes in the tenant's lease agreement said that the building super had the right to inspect the apartment at any time, so we had decided to take a chance.

At about 10:00 P.M., the black-clad group started to arrive, as couples, groups, and singles. I expected to see a freak show of wild leather-clad S&M types, leftover punks, and a host of Goth-culture Marilyn Manson wannabes. But those who entered 7S were mostly subdued looking people, albeit many dressed in black, but a number of them clad in what I can only describe as vintage clothing—neat, but definitely from a bygone era. They all entered in a very orderly way and there was no evidence of any sacrificial animals of any kind. I have been privy to Santería rituals in New York where animal sacrifice was performed as part of a religious ceremony. But if these people were in fact Satanists who were indeed perform-ing blood sacrifices in a residential building, we would have some recourse to oust the disturbing tenants, even if that was only a ruse to eliminate some other-worldly presence. But there was no evidence of any animal except the large black chow that was greeted cheerfully by the guests. I was a bit suspicious when I heard the dog called "Zazel," the name of an obscure demon.

The time moved quickly as I eyeballed the characters attending the gathering. I counted eleven people—that meant thirteen in total with the Hastingses, the preferred number of a witch's coven. And just as Aggie had described, at midnight the chatter and the clinking of glasses ceased. The apartment fell silent for a few moments. So silent in fact I briefly thought everyone might have left. But then I heard the sound of a gong being struck. It resonated three times and then fell silent. I have to admit I felt odd in my enclosed space. Odd, as though something or someone—like a fog—had entered not only the apartment down the hall, but the entire building.

The next thing I heard was a man's voice reciting. He was definitely delivering some kind of homily because I heard the guests respond in unison in a hushed tone. Shortly after the ceremony began, a strong odor of incense wafted into my room. I recognized it as predominantly frankincense with a hint of sulfur. This combination in itself made me wonder whether it had been deliberately combined as some blasphemous concoction, considering frankincense is used in Roman Catholic ceremonies.

I adjusted the dials on my listening and recording device so I could pick up the ritual clearly. Oddly enough, the recording perfectly stored the following:

> I command you, O all demons dwelling in these parts, or in what part of the world soever ye may be, whatsoever power may be given you by the powerful Principality of the abysses, both general and special demons, whether dwelling in the East, West, North or South, do our bidding this night. We summon ye too, O Master of Darkness, Prince of Light, Ruler of the Earth and Nine Gates to come and take the form of your earthbound servant.

At this point, the recording stopped, although I know the machine was running and fully charged. It had uncannily recorded only a small portion of the ceremony that I could hear completely as I eavesdropped from my closet. I remembered that the homily and responses grew louder as the ceremony continued. For nearly half an hour, I continually heard the words, "Hail Satan," in a loud group voice By this time, the strong smell of incense had me slightly woozy and somewhat nauseous. I think I drifted off into a nap or short sleep because I recall waking abruptly to the party sounds once again coming from 7S. Apparently, the ceremony was over and the revelry had started again. But this time the party sounds were different. I could hear distinct female voices giggling and footsteps running around the apartment. At first, the sounds of sexual moans and groans that I thought were my imagination became very clear. There seemed to be a full-blown orgy going on in 7S.

I began to hear screams of pleasure and what sounded like the slapping of flesh. There was now distinct music being played—a classical piece that I couldn't place but it was definitely a rhythmic, lusty composition that was whipping the guests into a frenzy. The orgy lasted several hours. I could see from under the front door that the rooms were illuminated with candlelight and my camera caught an occasional glimpse of shadows that flickered eerily on the hallway floor. In between the classical music, I could hear the banging of the gong . . . then silence . . . then the gong again in what I imagined was probably a sexual act viewed collectively by the group. It's legendary for Satanists to use sex as a powerful magical stimulus and catalyst for casting spells. My guess was that the lull in the action was the sexual union of two members in a spell-casting exercise.

Fortunately, my unexplained nap allowed me to last through the night so I could observe the guests as they left shortly before sunrise. To my amazement, none of the departing Satanists looked as though they had just completed a night of debauchery. None looked disheveled, drunk, or even tired for that matter. Their dress was as immaculate as when they first arrived and they all bid their hosts, the Hastingses, a pleasant good day as though they had just visited for an afternoon cup of coffee. They all shook hands and patted Zazel on the head. Some even hugged the dog's neck in what I thought was an over-the-top show of affection for an animal that most of the guests probably didn't see all that regularly.

In a twenty-four-hour corner coffee shop a few doors down from the building, I went over the evidence I had gathered. It was clear to me that the event I had witnessed the night before was not simply a cocktail party but was a magical ritual with a decidedly black-magic or left-hand-path bent. There is little that can be done when people have ceremonies in their own apartments aside from complaining to the authorities about noise or the possibility of assault, so the problem was really in what the tenants had been experiencing and attributing to the Hastingses. What made the case more difficult was that the Hastingses had lived in the building for many years with no problems. They were always thought of as somewhat eccentric, but never a problem.

It occurred to me that the building itself may have been the cause of the paranormal events—Sadie's bugs, the odors, banging hallway doors, and the dog's changing eyes—and that the Hastingses' dark leanings could have been the catalyst that put the weird events into motion. Most practitioners of the occult rarely perform rituals in the correct prescribed manner, usually opting to modify the magic to suit their tastes and whims. Historically, this has been disastrous, resulting in horrific physical assaults and sometimes even explosions, especially in cases where would-be sorcerers attempt to conjure demons to do their bidding. So, I wondered if something might have gone awry in the Hastingses' apartment that set off disturbances throughout the building. It was time to talk to the Hastingses and get to the bottom of their satanic soirees.

I was pleased that the Hastingses were open to discussing the matter with me, in fact, they even expressed delight that I might want to talk to them about what I described as "strange things" happening in their building. They were both dressed in black pants and shirts when they invited me into their apartment one Saturday evening at 9. I was immediately struck by the number of occult and horror movie objects evident in their kitchen, the first room I saw as I entered the apartment. What was particularly obvious were the satanic objects d'art that seemed to be everywhere. There were dolls, statues, magnets, signs, and a number of books on horror and the occult. I've seen every manner of weird house and apartment during my investigations and although the accoutrements of the Hastingses' apartment were indeed devilish, I didn't pick up on any foreboding or negative energy vibes that are usually associated with a malevolent presence or negative disturbance. In fact, the surroundings were quite homey, despite the furnishings and the lack of natural light.

I explained the neighbors' problems and concerns about demons and curses, which the Hastingses laughed off as hysterical rumors from "old women who don't know what to do with their time." And I was surprised when I asked them point blank if they were Satanists. "Yes, we are. We are members of a satanic church," Arthur said without flinching. He added that he was aware of the "curse" thrown at Sadie and that his fellow Satanist liked to "spook nosey people." "It's just Andrew fooling around," he said.

After some conversation about the rituals they perform for their religion and their philosophy of hurting no one unless defending themselves (which sounded perfectly in line with most people's philosophies), I was convinced that if they were guilty of conjuring a demonic presence it must have been done accidentally. However, both Arthur and Caroline were well versed in the magical arts, so I doubted that they had errored in their spell casting.

The couple did admit to recently having ceremonies conducted in their apartment because it was "their turn" as they progressed in the organization. And I was a bit shocked and embarrassed when they told me that they were well aware that I was spying on them. "We're used to being outcasts and people prying," Caroline said. "People just don't like anything or anyone who's not like them. They're all sheep and they want everyone to be sheep."

I left the Hastingses' apartment, satisfied that if they were responsible for the strange phenomena, it was a product of some paranormal anomaly and not deliberate. They were charming and gracious and actually invited me to sit in on a ritual in the near future. Of course, this didn't explain any of the paranormal events or the bugs in Sadie's place, but it wasn't the first time a case has gone unexplained.

As I left, I shook both of their hands and bent down to pat Zazel's head good-bye. I wasn't sure, but I remembered one of the tenants saying that one of the building's mysteries was how the dog's eyes changed from black to green whenever it was seen outdoors. But as I peered into the dog's eyes that stared at me as if human, the eyes were neither black *nor* green. Zazel's eyes were distinctly *brown*!

Epilogue

I learned that the disturbances finally stopped at the building about a month after my investigation when Aggie called to say hello. She said that everything now seemed back to normal and although the Hastingses still lived in 7S, the parties had stopped. I asked if anything else changed since I left and after a few moments of thought, Aggie said, "Well, not much . . . except that big black dog in 7S isn't there anymore. Someone said it ran away."

6.

The Computer
That Stole Souls

Peter and Gary were the owners of Digital Doctors computer repair service in a small New England town. It was one of the few such places in their area that actually made house calls to the technologically inept or phobic. The brothers would go to a home or office, try to figure out what was wrong with a person's machine, and if they could they'd repair it on the spot—a long forgotten style of service that harkened back to the days of medical doctor house calls and even TV repair services. So, when they got the call from Charles Higgins, they didn't think twice about visiting his home, and according to the brothers, they felt good that they were able to help people in their community and have a business at the same time. In Higgins's case, the call was especially fulfilling to the pair because they liked the idea that a senior citizen, an eighty-one-year-old widower, actually used a computer, and they were curious as to how technically proficient the old gent really was.

I called the brothers' store after I received a note from them saying they had seen an article on X-Investigations in one of their wives' magazines. They told me a bizarre tale of a "haunted or possessed" computer that they feared actually stole people's souls and infiltrated their lives. I admit that the Digital Doctor brothers' story sounded like an episode of the *Twilight Zone*, but that's what made it so much more appealing to me than the typical haunting or poltergeist tale.

Peter started his eerie recollection of the events by explaining that their service truck had rolled up to old man Higgins's house around 5:30 P.M. one November afternoon in 1997. Of course, it was typically gloomy, cold, and dark, but it was the last call of the day on the brothers' schedule. At least it would probably be an easy repair. How complicated could an eighty-one-year old's computer problem be? Peter thought to himself, so the job would no doubt be an easy end to the day. Higgins lived in a large frame house in serious disrepair. The house needed fixing a lot more than any computer did, and Peter made a mental note to pass on his handyman buddy's telephone number. When they walked up the creaking front stairs and peered through the glass panes of the huge wooden front door, the house was so dark inside that the brothers at first thought no one was home. But they spotted a dim light coming from a far-off corner in the back of the house. Gary tried the doorbell but heard no ringing, so he knocked on the door first gently and then pounding, figuring the old guy was hard of hearing. Higgins finally shuffled to the door, opened it a crack, and asked the brothers if they were the "computer geeks." Peter and Gary were both amused and a little surprised by the senior's terminology. "He was quite an amusing old guy. He was far more hip than we ever imagined and he knew quite a bit about his computer, despite the fact that it was an original Apple Macintosh machine with only 128K capacity—a relic in the market nowadays. Frankly, if we knew it was that dated we would have never bothered to come out, but Higgins simply said he had an 'Apple system' that needed a lot of work."

The brothers entered the dark old house and followed Higgins to the back where he had a musty smelling study set up with a chair, a desk, a standing floor lamp, and the blue glow from the Apple computer that supplied the only light in the room. As they moved closer to the desk, Peter and Gary were "creeped out" by how the computer seemed to dominate the space.

They later agreed that it was just an illusion because the screen had been the main source of light in an otherwise huge, dark space. But once the brothers started connecting the machine to a death and the odd occurrences in their own lives, they wondered whether their first impression might have been some sort of warning from a supernatural source.

They asked Higgins where he had gotten such an old machine. He explained that it had been given to him by Silka, his deceased wife's friend after she was "having problems" with it. "Yeah, Silka was real anxious to get rid of the computer. She said she got it from one of the kooky friends she hung around with. She was one of those psychic types, always runnin' around with crazy witches and such," old Higgins told them.

He then described how the computer was "actin' funny," not shutting down when he'd type in the command, turning itself on in the middle of the night, and most peculiar was how it would pop up Web pages from the Internet that Higgins said he never searched. "I know it's an old machine, but it's doin' stuff that I never tell it to do, which just ain't natural," Higgins explained. "You geeks gotta take her outta here and fix 'er up 'cause I ain't gotta lot of time left and there's lots I wanna see on the Internet before I go. And it ain't all this stuff about black magic and weird hoodoo that this Mac keeps poppin' up on the screen from the Internet either."

Despite the fact that the machine really couldn't be fixed and their polite explanation to Higgins that maybe he should just buy a new computer, the Digital Doctors decided that they would at least go through the motions, take the computer to the shop, and then call the old guy and tell him they couldn't fix it. Gary said to me that what he really wanted to do was just give Higgins a refurbished machine they had in the shop as a replacement and dump the old Mac because it was virtually worthless. But oddly enough, when they were leaving, Higgins said something to them that started them thinking there was a lot more to the computer's strange behavior than some technical glitch or perhaps Higgins's mistakes. "Okay boys, be careful with 'er. She tells me things that come true. Things that are gonna happen and then they do. And some things I don't really wanna hear, too—some scary things. But it told me something recently that's the most important thing I ever heard, but I ain't heard it all yet. So you boys fix it up soon. Ya know I ain't gotta lot a time left, like I told you. And that computer's got a mind of its own."

The Possession

The old Mac computer sat on the workbench of Digital Doctors for about a week. The brothers were too busy to deal with it, and they contemplated calling old Higgins and telling him it couldn't be fixed, delivering their refurbished machine to him, and calling it a day. But by the middle of week two, they began to get suspicious as to why Higgins hadn't inquired about his machine since he had seemed so anxious to have it repaired and to get the "answer" he was looking for. They really didn't believe the Mac was communicating with the old gent, dismissing his beliefs as some senile leanings, but they did feel he was sincere about wanting the machine back. Peter decided to take the "new" computer over to the house and explain the switch to Higgins. He drove up at the end of the workday and grabbed the refurbished machine out of the back of his truck. Peter noticed something hanging on Higgins's front door and his worst suspicions were confirmed as he got closer. A purple-bowed death wreath hung on the front door, an uncommon sight nowadays, but still traditional in their small community. Peter put the computer on the porch floor and read the notice tacked on the brown door that said that Higgins had died the prior week. Peter was saddened but not shocked, considering Higgins's age.

The next morning, glancing at the old Mac sitting on the workbench, Peter told Gary about Higgins's death. He told me that he was curious about the machine and powered it up just to see if it had any life left. The old Apple icon appeared and to Peter's surprise the machine seemed to be in good working condition. Peter thought the machine might be a good computer for his nine-year-old son Robbie to learn on, so he called his wife and told her to drop the boy off at the shop after school that day so he could become familiar with the Mac. Robbie was enthusiastic about having his own machine to use and Peter didn't have to worry about him breaking it. The boy was familiar with the basics. He even knew how to open files and move documents. But what Peter told me next was something he thought was peculiar even for an old computer. Whenever Robbie tried to open a file, it wouldn't respond except for one file labeled "Magus." But that was the least of the machine's weird behavior. Peter recalled how Higgins had complained about the computer having a mind of its own and opening pages about magic and witchcraft, but what he saw in the file labeled "Magus" that his son opened on the small screen completely freaked him out. The first page contained what looked like instructions for a ritual of some kind. There were arcane symbols and incantations that spoke of the afterlife and the "hand of glory"—which I knew from occult lore to be the primary ingredient in necromantic workings or magical spells to raise the dead. The "hand of glory" is traditionally the severed hand of a criminal corpse, usually one who has been hanged until dead. The hand is preserved and said to have incredibly potent occult power.

As if this wasn't disturbing enough, especially since Peter exposed it to his young son, but on the last page of the file he saw a name in large letters that was the obvious focal point of the spell. It read RANDOLPH HIGGINS—the old man's name.

At this point in the brothers' story, I was intrigued but not interested enough to devote my time to them because I really didn't think there was anything that could be considered paranormal or occult-based aside from the necromantic computer files. These might have been nothing more than files kept by an individual interested in the occult. And the fact that Higgins's name was in the ritual instructions could have been his own doing. Much stranger things have been discovered in people's computer files, I reasoned. I pressed the brothers for something much more unusual that might warrant my investigation. And I got it. Peter told me that next to Higgins's name was the date November 9, 1997. That was the day Higgins died.

My first thought was that Higgins's death was a suicide because that would explain the date and that Higgins himself could have entered it into the document. But Peter and Gary said they had checked with the local coroner and the old man had died of heart failure with no indication of suicide. But this possible coincidence alone wasn't what spurred the brothers to seek outside help. After some time passed and the Higgins mystery was just about forgotten, Robbie continued to use the computer in what Peter described as bordering on an obsessive way. "He would run to the shop from school and get right on the machine, sometimes staying on it for three hours or more before we went home to dinner. At first, we were happy that he showed such interest, but he had access to computers before and never exhibited so much enthusiasm and intense concentration," Peter said. He told me that at dinner one evening they had asked Robbie why he loved working on the old Mac so much. At first, he'd been reluctant to explain, but after some prodding by his parents Robbie told them that the machine told him to promise not to say anything to anyone about their "secret." Now annoyed at their child's odd behavior and reticence, they pressured Robbie to come clean. Peter said their son finally told them that the computer wrote his name by itself on files in the machine. "But I wasn't supposed to tell that it talks with me because something bad might happen," he told his parents.

This alone was odd but still not bizarre. Some children do have intense imaginations. But the day after Peter's son confessed to his strange relationship with the Mac, a "bad thing" did in fact happen. Riding his bicycle home from school,

Robbie was struck by a car and fell into a coma. Was this another coincidence? Peter turned on the old Mac and frantically searched for the files his son said it had created in the machine. Chills ran down his spine when he saw a page that was similar to the page with Higgins's name and day he died. This time it had Robbie's name on the page and the date was the day Robbie was struck by the automobile.

With the revelation of Peter's son's accident, what could have been coincidence took on a decided air of mystery for me. If there wasn't something supernatural occurring in the town, there could have been a cruel hoax being played on the Digital Doctor brothers and part of X-Investigations' charter was to expose scams as much as solve occult cases. So, I made arrangements to visit the New England town to investigate how an old computer could possibly have the date of its owner's death *before* the man died and what the occult necromantic connection might be. Was this what Higgins was so eager to learn from the machine? Was he an occult practitioner or the victim of some malevolent force? I was on another adventure that this time bridged the world of the occult with the world of technology.

Before I left New York, I asked Vincent to have some of the staff at the detective agency do some background work for me so I'd be prepared when I went up north. Vincent advised me that most cases that turn out to be hoaxes usually begin with someone who has a history of scamming and grifting, so I wanted to be prepared if this was the case. And although there didn't seem to be any monetary angle involved, there had been a death and an accident—signs that could be the work of a seriously demented con man. I managed to find out the names of all of the parties involved with the "possessed" computer and they all checked out clean. The one question mark was Silka, Higgins's wife's friend, who had given the old man the Macintosh computer in the first place. Silka had some minor charges on her record concerning her involvement with unlawful gatherings in nearby woods (usually witchcraft or Wiccan ceremonies) and a charge for grave robbing that was lessened to a misdemeanor with the explanation that she had been guilty of participating in a rather intense Halloween party scavenger hunt. Although Silka's record appeared innocent enough on paper, the two offenses were hallmarks of occult involvement. Her record, coupled with the current events, pointed to Silka as the first person I needed to speak with concerning Higgins's mysterious computer and Peter's son's accident.

When I arrived at the Digital Doctors' shop, Gary met me and explained that Peter was at the hospital visiting his son, who was happily beginning to show signs of improvement. Gary said he was pleased to see me because things were getting "very strange" ever since the old computer entered the shop. He told me that he and his brother were apprehensive about discussing their suspicions. "We talk to each other about this damn thing and how we think it's evil. But then we think we're going nuts. But there are just too many coincidences to blow it off," Gary said. I mentioned that I thought the Higgins event was strange but could have been a coincidence, but I agreed that the boy's accident was extremely odd and that's when I got spooked. Gary then surprised me by saying that there was even more to the story. "Since you spoke to Peter, we started experiencing what the old man was telling us. We really took this thing apart and looked into every file on its drive. But there's weird stuff going on. We shut the computer off at night but then it's on when we get into the office in the morning. We close down a file and then find it open again minutes later. And one night I swear I unplugged the son of a bitch only to find it plugged back in and turned on within hours. It's just too bizarre," Gary said.

I asked if there could be some technical glitch or power surge type of anomaly that could make the computer act so crazy, but Gary assured me that they had checked the machine out thoroughly and there was nothing electronically wrong with it. The old Mac did indeed appear to have a mind of its own. But my inquiry was far more concerned with the magical files that contained Higgins's and the boy's name. And, of course, what Silka's role was in this macabre Mac. I suspected that Silka was either the source of the computer's malevolent behavior or at the very least a significant piece of the puzzle. Gary was right . . . there were far too many unexplained events to chalk up to coincidence.

The Soul Snatcher

I discovered from town records that Silka lived in the oldest section of town, and I arranged for a cab to take me to her home the following morning. She had no telephone number listed, so I was forced to arrive unannounced. Her home, much like Higgins's, was old, in disrepair, and generally creepy. The thicket that lined the front walk was so overgrown that the concrete pathway virtually disappeared. I was pricked at the ankle a number of times as I walked toward the front door. Whenever I begin an investigation, I immediately look for telltale signs of occult activity in places most people would never think of looking, especially outdoors. I check gardens for growing mandrake root or mugwort (known ingredients in spell

casting) and other herbs, and I look for symbols over door-
ways and statues and effigies, which are always dead give-
aways of particular persuasions. Animals, too, can sometimes
be indicators of the practices of the dark arts. Most people
immediately think of black cats as witches' familiars, but the
presence of other animals such as an unusually large number
of toads or exotic birds are often clues.

Silka's house was clean—from the outside anyway. She
answered the door, opened it about three inches, just enough
to see who I was, and suspiciously asked what I wanted. I
explained that I was investigating Higgins's death. Once we
got past the "are you a cop" banter and she understood that I
was a paranormal investigator, she allowed me to come into
her home. She was in her mid-sixties and dressed in flowing
silky reds and purple wraps. It was hard to tell if what she
wore was a garment or just yards of material wrapped around
her body. Her long silver-and-black hair reached down to the
middle of her back and she wore an ankle bracelet with a bell
on it that rang with each step she took, making her sound
like a common house cat on the prowl. As I expected, Silka
had a number of books on the occult in plain view and she
wasn't shy about her avocation as a psychic medium and
channeler. She told me that she was very friendly with Higgins's wife, Theresa, who often consulted her on psychic matters and correspondence with relatives who had passed on.
She said she was very fond of Theresa and is still in touch
with her "on the other side."

When the subject turned to old man Higgins himself,
Silka was visibly upset about his death. I asked her if she was
comfortable with the report that he had died of natural
causes. At first she nodded. I noticed some apprehension
when I told her that his name and date of death was found on

the old computer of his. I then asked if she was the person who in fact had given him the old Mac. "Yes, I gave him the machine, but I did tell him that it was to be used just for fun. I know he got a little obsessed with it. Theresa told me so, before she died. But I warned her that he should be careful with some of the things that were left on the computer," Silka said. I asked what she had left on it. She replied that it was none of her doing and that was how she had received it—with the magic ceremonies on its hard drive. "Some of the files are very harmless—child's play sort of magic. But there are also very dangerous spells and ceremonies on that machine. Necromantic spells to raise the dead for one . . . and even some more serious black magic. It's the reason I got rid of it, to tell you the truth," Silka admitted.

That revelation took me by surprise. Apparently, Silka was very much aware that Higgins's computer contained a number of magical ceremonies and instructions that she thought could be dangerous. I asked her how she knew about the files and she said because of how she obtained the computer in the first place. One of Silka's past lovers, a serious practitioner in the occult arts by the name of Morton, had been the original owner. Silka revealed that Morton was obsessed with the art of necromancy and explained that he even had her dig up bodies so he could use the severed hands in his rituals (thus explaining her police record). She explained that for years Morton had devoured every black magic grimoire, book, and bit of information he could find. He traveled the world in search of the right ingredients and combination of spell and incantation that would give him power over death. "I loved Morton, but I was also very frightened of him. He was a powerful magician—a mage—in the dark arts who was so focused on piercing the other side that his house was literally filled to the ceiling with books and information. He spent almost all of his family fortune on obtaining these works, and he experimented for years," Silka said.

I asked her how Morton's interest in the occult was related to the strange computer actions. Silka told me that Morton had so much material that when he learned how to use the computer he began to transfer it into the machine. But she added that he only included the most potent workings and spells in the computer, sort of a digital safe to store his most valuable items. As he became more and more proficient in using the Mac, Morton pored over it for hours on end, studying the arcane texts and mysterious writings. Even though the machine was archaic by today's standards, Morton did not trust moving any of his precious files to another machine, so with the advent of the Internet he had it updated so he could communicate with the entire world by computer. Silka said that the Internet connection virtually chained Moron to the Mac. "He rarely left his house. He was able to find dark magic information from all over the world, and what was even more frightening was that he could talk with others who performed black magic." She went on to explain how Morton first joined Internet chat rooms and then went on to instant messaging students of the occult all over the world. He joined a circle of global magicians that had been gathering knowledge for thousands of years and had transferred the dark knowledge to a major database that could only be accessed by members of the group. Apparently, the group admitted only the most serious adepts who demonstrated expert knowledge in many magical arts and could pass a stringent test. Silka said that Morton did not leave the computer for days during the testing process and when he completed it, he looked drained and sickly. "That's not all . . . it cost him thousands of dollars to belong to that group. He lost a lot of money. But he lost a lot more," Silka said.

"A lot more what," I asked.

"Morton lost his soul to that group and that machine. He was never the same afterward."

I pressed Silka to tell me why she had given old man Higgins the computer if she knew it contained such dangerous information. It especially puzzled me considering that Higgins's wife was such a close friend. It turned out that Silka wanted the machine out of her house to avoid temptation. She was no stranger to the occult arts, having dabbled in spells for her own personal gain. She was tempted to join Morton's group to discover why he was so obsessed. "For Morton to be that involved—for any person to be so intent and dedicated to something—the payoff must have been enormous. The computer was constantly staring me in the face. I turned it on many times with the intention of uncovering Morton's mysteries, but I never went all the way. I knew it would destroy me," Silka said.

Of course, I then asked why she had given it to Higgins and she admitted that she thought he was just a simple old man, and without the knowledge or inclination to pursue magic and the unknown, he would have used it as nothing more than a new gadget. "Higgins loved old radios and such— you know—gadgets. I thought it would be harmless in his hands; after all it *was* just a computer. Morton on the other hand, had used it as means to an end, and I knew I could too. That's why I *really* got rid of it. But for Higgins, it was just a toy," Silka reiterated. I thought to myself: Yeah, a toy . . . seems like this toy's more like a loaded gun.

The troubling investigation now began to make some sense. The computer was obviously the catalyst for the strange events, and my common sense told me that Higgins and perhaps the Digital Doctor brothers were victims of some kind of damaging rumor that often takes on a life of its own. They all may have heard the strange stories of Morton's quest and somehow psychologically transferred the evil to themselves as a bizarre sort of self-fulfilling prophecy. But my theory couldn't explain how the Morton tales could have been potent enough to actually kill Higgins. And what's more, could a case of such scattered suggestion work on the mind of an innocent young boy as well? The other possibility, the one that I naturally resisted, was that the machine itself had been "infected" by Morton's necromantic workings and harbored a malevolent force capable of damaging the lives of its owners. The latter seemed far-fetched, even to someone like me, who has investigated numerous paranormal and occult cases.

I had never been faced with the possibility of an inanimate object actually causing someone harm, so I shelved those theories and went back to doing some hard-nosed investigating, which I believed at the very least would help the brothers find some peace of mind. But one question kept creeping into my mind: How did Higgins's and the injured boy's names and dates appear in the machine's files? The boy could have entered a date as a reminder of something he had to do on that day, and so could have Higgins, for that matter. But that didn't explain the coincidence of the style—both files simply listed the full name and then the date, almost like a log-in of sorts. I decided the answer would be to go into the machine's hard drive and check the actual dates of when the ill-fated users actually entered their names. In this way, I could see if the names were entered after the events as some kind of hoax. I was sure the Digital Doctors were capable of cracking into the machine and figuring it out, so I called Gary at home as soon as I reached my hotel room.

"We tried ... that was the first thing we did," Gary answered the second I asked him to check out my idea. He went on to tell me that because the machine was so old no one knew how to go back and search the internal brain. "No one remembers that old Apple operating system around here. We even called Apple and they couldn't help us with it. Remember, that machine's a dinosaur. It's amazing that it still works and whomever had it rigged to run on the Internet corrupted its original internal workings anyway. We thought of that right away ... how could the name and dates be there and coincide with the tragedies ... but it's still a mystery," Gary said.

It occurred to me after speaking with Gary that I had never learned what ultimately became of Morton, so I visited Silka again the next morning. She was very polite despite my once again unannounced arrival and questioning. Although she was in her twilight years, Silka was still flirtatious and she was obviously happy to have a male caller. We also hit it off because of our affinity for the occult and she seemed genuinely pleased to be able to converse about the dark arts with some-one who knew her language. "This town could be so dreadfully boring ... so mundane, most of the townspeople even freak out at Halloween if things get too spooky," Silka told me.

After some hot tea, I got around to asking Silka about Morton. She said that she was wondering when I was going to inquire about his demise, and she went on to tell the story of how one evening after weeks of intense study and magical workings Morton had collapsed in his chair and died of what the coroner listed as heart failure due to extreme exhaustion and dehydration. He had been reading from his magical books and checking the Internet, constantly running back and forth from his library to the machine. "I went over to his house because I hadn't seen him for days and I was worried. I knew he could be absorbed for hours, but this was suspiciously too long, even for Morton," Silka said.

When she had arrived at Morton's home, the only light she could see shone from his attic, where he kept the computer. She could see his shadow bouncing off of the walls and flashing from one end of the room to the other as he frantically checked pages in the books and scrolled down the screen of the old Mac that had become his gateway to the world's entire knowledge of the arcane. Silka again told me that Morton's ultimate quest was to gain immortality . . . to learn how he could harness the necromantic workings in a way that would prolong his life and perhaps cheat death itself. "Most people think this is Hollywood horror movie stuff. But there are many true believers, especially us older types, who will do anything to stay alive. Morton wanted nothing more than to be immortal. He believed if he could learn how to bring things back to life, he could bring himself back to life if he should die."

As Silka recounted the night Morton died, I began to understand why she was so frightened about having the computer in her possession. The old magician ironically worked himself to death in an effort to live forever. Silka went on to explain how she called to him many times but he didn't answer, she just heard him running back and forth, books being dropped, and a maelstrom of activity. "Then the ceremony began," Silka said.

Morton apparently discovered what he was looking for in his books and on the Internet, and a black magic ritual ensued. Silka took a deep breath and was at first reluctant to describe what happened next, but I assured her that I have heard it all and have often been an eye witness to what most people would consider extremely bizarre and harrowing. She agreed to fill me in and told me how Morton's house suddenly became quiet. There was no noise coming from the attic but she knew he was preparing for a ritual because the smell of incense began wafting down the stairs and she could hear a low chanting coming from the top of the stairs that she couldn't immediately identify but described as "an ominous religious ceremony in fractured Latin." Silka remained quietly mesmerized by Morton's chanting that became increasingly louder. I listened intently as she described how the house seemed to "be unaffected by the present time" and had gotten very cold. "I turned on the one floor lamp in the living room so I could at least see my hand in front of my face, but let me tell you it was very eerie in that house during Morton's ritual. It went on for at least forty minutes. I couldn't wait any longer, I had to leave. I just left the food I brought over on his coffee table and I went home. I still saw his shadow in the window as I walked way so I knew he was okay. But then I heard the bad news the next day . . . that Morton passed on the night before," Silka concluded.

The case now took on a new interest for me. Morton's intense involvement in the occult fascinated me and I wanted to learn as much about him as about the mysterious computer itself. I reasoned that if I could learn enough about Morton, perhaps I could make some sense out of the hold, if any, his computer had on its recent users or perhaps understand how Morton's legend could have affected the townspeople in some mass hypnotic phenomenon.

I asked the Digital Doctor brothers if I could use the computer myself the next day. I was spending too much time on the case and Silvana repeatedly phoned me from New York about a backlogged investigation involving a woman who claimed to be sexually possessed by a demon. Well, that sounded like fun, but first things first. The brothers warned me that the machine continued to "act up" and that it was risky to fool around with it, but I knew it was the only way I was going to satisfy my curiosity about the old Mac and Morton the mage. I pored over Morton's old files—there were hundreds of arcane and esoteric texts transferred from books and files from every continent—some dating back nearly a thousand years that I knew were the property of the Vatican and forbidden to be viewed by anyone outside of the Church. I saw magical texts and excerpts from *The Grand Grimoire*, *The Grimoire of Pope Honorius*, and a number of rituals in languages of which I had no idea of the origin. There was also Morton's private diary that described his studies but was written in a code of his own that was difficult to understand. What I could discern from Morton's files was that through ritual and the use of a *different living body* or *living tissue* he had somehow discovered how to transfer the "life essence" to a body after it died. It became clear that Morton was attempting to transfer his soul to another, perhaps younger living body during the intense ritual Silka described. But apparently the intensity of the magic was too much for him and he never completed the task. Or did he? And who was the unwilling victim?

This still didn't explain the old Mac and its role in Higgins's death or the boy's injury. Morton owned the machine, and it was a device to hold information. So I racked my brain as to how these happenings were linked, if at all.

My cell phone rang the next morning and I expected to hear Silvana again demanding that I get back to the office, but it was Peter, and he sounded cheerful. He said he wanted to let me know that Robbie had come out of his coma early that morning. He asked if I discovered anything on the Mac and I told him that all I found was that Morton, the original owner, had some pretty bizarre magical information stored on it and it did seem to flicker on and off for no reason. I asked about his son and he said he seemed to be fine, but he mentioned that he had expected the boy to ask where he was or what had happened to him when he awoke. But instead, Peter said that he had asked a strange question.

"What was it?" I asked.

"Well," Peter said, "he asked if I knew anything about some pope named Amorious or Honorius, or something like that."

Epilogue

I called Silvana on the way home and told her the whole story. I asked her if she thought Morton managed to use the old Macintosh computer as some paranormal conduit to store his soul until he could then possess a living body. Was Higgins's body too old and unable to stand the stress? Was Peter's son too strong and innocent? She answered, "Robert, computers are thinking machines. They are becoming another kind of intelligence—maybe not artificial intelligence at all. And maybe they can have a soul, too. Maybe Morton's soul."

7.

The Succubus

Owners of detective agencies get a lot of strange phone calls. Some are odd inquiries, some are threats, and others are more mundane "follow my cheating husband" calls. But when Vincent got the call for X-Investigations one Wednesday afternoon that caused even him to do a double take and blush deep red, I knew our next case would be anything but ordinary.

Vincent called me into his office and said that in his twenty-five years as a private detective he'd been involved in a number of cases dealing with sexual situations and peccadilloes, even some cases where he had to stake out wild sex parties and private clubs. But in all that time, he had never heard of a husband complaining that his wife was an insatiable sexual beast who was totally out of control. "I tell you, Bob, he was ranting about what a sexual animal his wife is. At first, I just wanted to hang up on the guy because I thought he was a nut—and we get these nut balls calling all of the time. But he said his referral was a friend of mine—a major banker here in the city that I've known for years—so I kept listening. He told me name was Roger and his problem was that he couldn't keep up with his wife's demands in bed. So I thought to myself, that's the problem? Why didn't he call a sex therapist? Then he starts to tell me about how she's out of her mind with lust—seeking sex all over the city with men and women, groups, every type of crazy situation. And by now I'm thinking to myself that this is just one crazy horny woman."

I admit I was intrigued by the call from the desperate husband, although at first I thought it was probably one of Vincent's jokes and that the punch line was going to come any second. But I noticed an atypical concerned look in Vincent's eyes as he continued talking. His brow creased and his eyes became much more serious.

I asked, "So what happened? Another sex-crazed woman on the loose?"

"It's more than that. I've had those crazy cases before. And this is what's weird. It wasn't me he really wanted to talk to. It was you and the X team."

"The X team?" I asked, "How could we help a guy with a problem like that? What is she, possessed by a sex demon?" I asked sarcastically.

"That's exactly what this guy Roger claims. He said his wife's a sexual demon—she does strange things, his house is full of pornography and she wants to have sex with almost everyone she comes in contact with. She's totally out of control and he doesn't know where to turn. That's why he needs your help," Vincent said.

After we had a few laughs at the unfortunate husband's expense, I got serious about the case and asked Vincent if he could tell me any more details. He said that the problem had existed for about three months and at first Roger had demanded that his wife, Linda, see a psychologist and eventually a medical doctor and psychiatrist—all to no avail. The woman was getting progressively worse and her sexual problems were linked to even more disturbing behavior. Linda was performing what Roger described as "perverse" rituals using odd ingredients, candles, and weird chanting. "Bob, this poor guy even told me that his wife was doing crazy ceremonies in their basement totally in the nude and even mixing stuff in bowls that looked like, well . . . you know, ejaculations," Vincent said.

I expected when we started X-Investigations that we would see and hear of bizarre experiences from the people who sought our services. When dealing with the paranormal and the occult, it is not at all uncommon to meet the strangest people imaginable. We have investigated hauntings, curses, possessions, werewolves, vampires, and UFOs, and we have helped people who have not experienced the unexplainable but have been bilked by occult scam artists or phony psychics. Until Vincent told me about Roger's insatiable wife who was apparently affected by a sexual power that transcended normal boundaries, I thought I had heard it all. For someone to be so desperate that he had to contact a private investigator with a paranormal unit, Roger had to have had exhausted every traditional means of help. I had to know more, but I also had to be sure that what was troubling the woman fit into our investigation parameters. I asked Vincent to do some checking on Linda before we contacted Roger, just to be sure we weren't heading into some kind of setup the husband may have been planning to trap his cheating wife. Or worse, we didn't want to waste our time on a couple of bored well-to-do partners who wanted to have a little fun with the "ghost busters."

It took about a week, but Vincent's investigators verified all of Roger's claims and then some. A detailed report documented Linda's bizarre behaviors, from stalking sexual partners in the wee hours of the morning to masturbating in the back pews of a Roman Catholic church. Photos that accompanied the report showed Linda in the most outrageous and outlandish sexually provocative outfits. She was in her early thirties and very attractive. She wore revealing clothing—short, tight skirts and low-rise jeans that displayed part of her underwear. Her breasts were almost always in full view, jutting out of her blouse. Vincent's operative wrote that Linda often walked the streets late at night braless with her blouse wide open. She was arrested several times for indecent exposure and soliciting, but the hooker charges never stuck because she never asked for any money. I was glued to the findings and pored over the entire fifty-five-page report in minutes. The description of Linda's deviant behavior got even worse, depicting her urinating in the streets in full view of passers-by and driving her car in the nude past construction sites in the middle of the day in an effort to seduce the workers. A long-distance recording of her in the throes of passion contained foul-mouthed sexual requests from her sporadic lovers. Curiously, some of the recordings were in foreign languages that, according to Roger, Linda didn't speak.

The report also described how Linda would spend time in her basement almost every night of the week immediately after dinner. Despite the fact that she was continuing to have regular sexual relations with her husband, she wasn't satisfied.

Her exhausted husband would eat dinner, be lured into his bedroom by his wife whether in the mood or not, and forced to have sex night after night. In part, the report read:

> Roger was often reluctant to leave the dinner table. Linda would finish eating, leave the room, and return in negligees or just in her bra and panties, and she would then pull Roger by the arm into their bedroom. From all accounts, they would have sex for the better part of an hour. Auditory moans and screams of passion were common.

The "basement rituals" fascinated me most. Linda created an entire sexual playroom that contained sex toys, whips, chains, paddles, harnesses, contraptions, and mechanical devices for various pleasurable and sadomasochistic encounters. Vincent's operative's report continued:

> The makeshift dungeon was built in the center of what appears to be some kind of religious ritual chamber complete with stone altar and eight-foot-high wooden crucifix fitted with wrist and ankle straps. The windows are painted black to block any daylight from entering, the walls are painted a deep red with pornographic murals depicting nude people having sex with each other, in orgies and fornicating with goat-like creatures.

It sounded to me like Linda had read one too many books on Marquis de Sade and was playing out her wildest fantasies. But the ritual chamber spoke of more occult leanings, especially the stone altar and what the investigator described as "odd markings painted on the basement floor that appeared to be a form of hieroglyphics or a foreign code of some kind."

But few of the cases we've investigated contain allegations of anything truly "occult." I have been involved with countless cases of alleged witchcraft and people casting evil spells. But almost all of our findings conclude that the actual participants in the witchcrafts are simply poseurs—most never conduct rituals or cast spells. I thought the odd markings and stone altar in Linda's basement had been put there for effect—more as part of an elaborate psychodrama than with any real paranormal or occult intent. The only way X-Investigations could actually weed out the phonies from the real occultists was to interview them one on one. And I knew that in Linda's case this was going to be one of the most interesting interviews I had ever conducted. If she were simply using the occult trappings to mask her true intentions for the sake of her husband, I would see through that within the first few minutes of our conversation. And if she was simply an oversexed woman who believed she was suffering from nymphomania, I would suggest that she see a physician and a psychiatrist. But the long shot in this scenario was that Linda was actually using the occult to facilitate her sexual leanings or more disturbing, that some occult force was using her.

The Succubus

Linda agreed to meet me at the agency offices after hours one Monday evening. This was the only day of the week that her husband said she usually stayed home because the "pickings were thin" at the local meet markets. And interestingly enough, she was excited to be able to tell a stranger about her newfound lust. Roger had sheepishly told me that she was giving him graphic details about her most recent encounters and had said that whomever interviewed her was going to be in for the shock of his life when he heard what she had done. He told me of how she had now posted fully nude photos of herself on her Web site and that she planned to visit Los Angeles to audition for porn movies. "She even invited one of the producers from Chatsworth, California—the heart of the X-rated movie business—to come to New York and stay at our apartment. I see no end to this madness," Roger said. Linda didn't let up on her husband either. She told him that she had an even more bizarre story to tell her interviewer that even he would find beyond belief. Roger lowered his head as he told me that as Linda said this, she had a very strange look in her eyes. "She looked like a woman possessed, and that's not all. As she talked to me, her hand was in her panties and she was muttering something in what sounded like Latin and she was masturbating, for God's sake! I couldn't believe that she did that right in front of me! It freaked me out."

It freaked me out, too. At that point, I didn't know what to expect from my encounter with Linda other than she needed some kind of help. The comment about her speaking in Latin intrigued me, but I wondered whether that could be part of her play-acting.

Linda walked into my office dressed more conservatively than I had expected: she wore a basic blue business suit and tan sling-back high heels that accentuated her tall 5' 9" frame. She had the stature of a model, sleek and lean, and she walked with runway grace. She was very attractive with classic features and shiny, long black hair that, although unfashionable, suited her perfectly. On the street, one would have thought she was a successful advertising executive or perhaps a lawyer. But the swing in her walk belied any conservative leanings. Linda exuded a confidence and sexual prowess in just the way she walked. I imagined what she must have looked like when she was on the prowl dressed in her most revealing outfits. The way she looked she could have attracted almost any man or woman without much effort, with or without magical aids.

I was blunt with Linda. I told her that Roger had told me all about her wild sexual escapades and her defiance. I also told her that I knew all about her "not-so-secret" basement hideaway with its S&M paraphernalia and occult altar. I spoke for a good ten minutes straight, harshly elaborating on what she had done and saying that I thought that all of her magical and occult trappings were so much mumbo jumbo. I wanted to make it perfectly clear that I wasn't buying any paranormal excuses for her bizarre behavior and that she should end the charade and stop hurting the people she loved.

Linda let me rant without interruption, listening intently to my criticisms and remarks about her sexuality. I was prepared for her to lash out, asking who I thought I was to butt into her private life. Of course, I was going to use her husband as my reason for the inquiry but I didn't have to use that trump card. After I finished talking, Linda smiled and locked her green eyes on me. "Mr. Johnson," she said, "do you know that I have a mini vibrator inserted in my vagina and it's been turned on throughout your little diatribe? And I've also experienced an orgasm or two while you were lecturing me."

I admit it—I was caught completely off guard. I expected Linda to blast me and in fact was hoping that she would have grown so angry that she would wittingly or unwittingly betray the real reason behind her actions. But instead, the long shot that I had dismissed as a one-in-a-million possibility, began to emerge. Linda's breathing became more pronounced and heavy as she spoke. What started as a soft, seductive tone took on a gravely, guttered rasp. Linda's next outburst was even more shocking to me than her sexual comments. She leaned back in her chair, tossed her head back to loosen her hair, and began speaking in tongues.

Speaking in tongues means exactly that. A person speaks in foreign languages and occasionally in ancient or forgotten languages he or she has never spoken or heard before. Even the most talented con artist would have difficulty fooling trained investigators by faking different tongues. And from what I knew of Linda, she was basically a middle-class woman who never had been involved in a con game or had the benefit of world travel or schooling by which she might have learned multiple languages. And Linda's phrasing sounded perfect, strange in itself coming from a novice. But what really puzzled me was the pitch of her voice that changed as though there were another voice, or simultaneous voices, coming from her mouth. Each time she spoke, a different pitch and tone resonated, confirming in my mind that there was a lot more to Linda than a typical horny housewife.

I questioned her for the better part of an hour, asking why she was so obsessed with sex and why she had no concern for her husband or for what people thought of her lewd actions. Her comments shifted from being snide and seductive to almost pathetic and needy. One second Linda was leaning over, exposing her cleavage and telling me that pleasure was the only thing that mattered to her and the next moment she was holding her head in her hands and saying that she couldn't control herself. All at once she began to compose herself and told me that she felt she was out of control since the dreams began. I asked her what she meant and she explained that some months prior to her wild behavior she had been experimenting with some magic spells that she found in books her brother gave her on her birthday. Her brother, a construction worker, had been cleaning out an occult store called Magickal Childe near the Flatiron District in Manhattan after it had gone out of business. He found books buried behind some of the walls that were being gutted and thought Linda would enjoy them because of her interest in witchcraft and the occult. Linda told me that the books looked very rare and she pored over them for weeks. Part of the package her brother gave her contained a handwritten diary of sorts that diagramed certain spells. One spell in particular titled "To Summon Love Eternal" appealed to Linda, and after weeks of deliberation she finally summoned enough courage to try conducting the spell. She confessed that she had never before tried anything more than lighting a few candles, but the description of how an angelic being would actually visit her and bestow an incredibly loving experience seduced Linda into taking the chance on performing the magic.

Everything had gone fine when she prepared her magical circle in the basement of her home on the prescribed night. She had all the necessary candles lit, performed all of the purifying steps and movements, and made the small sacrifices of burnt offerings spelled out in the old diary. The burning incense filled the basement and her husband was out bowling that evening, so he wouldn't be alarmed by the odd odors emanating from his house. For over an hour, Linda followed each step of the intricate and grueling spell exactly as it was written, sitting dead center in her painted circle. She then described how the mix of smells and intense concentration made her light-headed and she began to swoon. "I remember that I was near the end of the spell and I began to feel dizzy. I then saw a very bright flash in front of my eyes and a shadowy figure that appeared to have a giant wingspan flashed in front of my eyes. Then I must have stumbled around and passed out because I awoke some twenty minutes later outside of the circle about three feet away from where I started the ritual," she said.

Linda went on to describe how she was so exhausted that she quickly bathed and went to bed before her husband arrived home. That's when the dream began. Linda told me she had experienced the most intensely vivid sexual dream she had in her entire life. In fact, she experienced such intense multiple orgasms throughout the night that she found it difficult to get out of bed the next morning. But the dream wasn't the most intriguing part of Linda's story. She told me about the lover in her dream, a huge male being who was human but much larger and who had giant wings. The being began touching and fondling her gently but then worked her into countless savage lovemaking sessions that all at once frightened and stimulated her in ways she had never before experienced. The winged being then told Linda that she was now a messenger of eternal lust and she was to deliver the sins of the flesh to all she met. "I was completely ravaged and spent. But I was so alive. I was exhilarated beyond belief, but I was also scared that I crossed boundaries—lewd, disgraceful boundaries that made me feel dirty and at the same time wonderfully sexy." Linda described how she awoke drenched in a satisfied sweat but still ready for more sex. "I felt the being's presence still with me . . . inside of me as though he were now part of me. My whole body ached for more. I was transformed into what I am now. I'm ashamed to say that I feel like a whore, but also like the most desired woman on earth. The dream . . . or the spell worked. And I love the sexual creature I've become," Linda said.

As she spoke, I began to hypothesize about the cause of Linda's strange behavior. I recognized that the spell she found in the book was designed to summon an entity of some kind—either an angel or a demon—perhaps an *incubus*—a male demon that infects human females with perverse lust and feeds off of the energy. I then recalled that the Latin word for nightmare—*incubo*—described intense erotic scenarios and a heavy feeling of something lying on the dreamer's body and could be a connection. Things were starting to fall into place. Her description of the ritual described elements of kabbalistic ritual magic with its prescribed protective circle and "Triangle of Art." These rituals were used to summon demons but are considered extremely dangerous, especially for the untrained magician. Because she was a novice at conducting spells, the intensity of the event probably caused her to stumble out of the circle. The magical circle drawn with the proper ingredients protects the magician from being attacked or possessed by the entity that's being summoned for whatever purpose. But apparently, Linda had not understood the importance of remaining confined in the secure area and allowed the entity to possess her. Father Sinistrari, a noted seventeenth-century demonologist, often described these types of demons as entities that take the body of humans to use as sexual conduits for copulating with other human beings. St. Augustine and St. Thomas Aquinas cen-turies before also believed in malevolent spirits usually called incubus (male) or succubus (female). I hypothesized that once the entity materialized, Linda somehow fell outside of the circle, allowing the demon to make contact with her. The ensuing erotic dream was not a dream at all but the actual experience of what I suspected to be an incubus who had entered Linda and transformed her into a kind of magnet for the sexual energy it fed on. Many occult scholars also believe that these demons collect the semen of humans to artificially inseminate other humans in order to produce giant demonic offspring. The female victim of an incubus herself becomes a succubus to prey on unknowing "sperm donors."

Linda left my office after nearly three hours of interview and discussion about her strange new sexual life. She was unapologetic and confident that whatever had made her change was improving her life and making her feel more of a woman than she had ever felt before. She made it clear to me that she had no intention of leaving Roger and that he was a "useful" person to keep her satisfied when she wasn't enjoy-ing her new "vast universe of pleasures." Before she left, I remembered that I had neglected to ask her about her reli-gious beliefs. Often, demons will purposely attack devoutly religious people—especially priests and nuns of the Roman Catholic faith—as a blatantly blasphemous gesture against God. The question stopped Linda in her tracks. "Funny you should ask that. Until my dream, I guess you could have con-sidered me a very religious woman. I was a practicing Catholic," she said.

"You *were* a Catholic?" I asked.

"Yes, that's right, I was. I no longer believe in such non-sense. In fact, for a short time after high school I actually attended retreats in upstate New York that prepared girls to become novice nuns. I thought that was what I was called to do. But now I see how foolish that was." As she was explaining her religious rebellion, I noticed that Linda was fidgeting with the necklace that hung down the front of her white satin blouse. I hadn't seen what it was before because it disappeared into the cleavage of her breasts, but now she slowly pulled out the necklace. At first, it looked like Catholic rosary beads, but then I noticed that they were not the typically round beads that connected a V-shaped path down to a crucifix. The beads were black and rough and looked like large dried peas. And between a number of the beads I could see tiny charms or trinkets. I didn't want to appear rude by staring, but I was transfixed by the neclace's odd makeup. When the necklace came into full view, I could see that the charms were miniature phallic symbols made of pewter. Some were larger than others, but they all represented the male sexual organ in fine detail. The odd "rosary" did, however, resemble traditional Catholic prayer beads but for one detail—the black crucifix at the end of the beads hung upside down.

Linda dangled the rosary in front of her chest. "So, you can see I was a good little girl for a long time, going to church and being pious and all that bullshit. But when I tasted the fruits of pure lust that's cleansed with fire, I realized not letting go was a fool's game. The only damnation is our hell here on earth. So that's why I had my shocking little satanic rosary here made up, to always remind me that my body is the only real temple and that the more I please myself, the happier I will be," Linda said.

She dangled the beads in front of me and for the first time I made eye contact with her that lasted for more than a split second. She began to move the rosary from hand to hand and brushed it across her blouse front closer and closer to her breasts. All the while, her eyes were glued to mine and I must admit that it was becoming difficult not to look at her. She was not only an attractive woman, but her gaze was more arresting than normal. I wasn't sure at that moment if my mind was beginning to run away with itself because of the interview we had concerning the powers of the succubus, or if this was nothing more than a seriously flirtatious moment. She began to massage her breasts, continuing to look at me seductively. Our eyes were locked but I could peripherally see both of her hands pressing and kneading her breasts that now appeared much larger than I first thought. The top button of her blouse came undone and her ample flesh was being pushed up and out of her bra as she cupped both breasts with her hands. I asked what she was doing and told her that I felt very uncomfortable. But as hard as I tried, I could not take my eyes away from hers. Her body was closer now and in what seemed to be a fraction of a second both of her breasts were now completely exposed with nothing blocking my view, aside from the blasphemous rosary.

"They're beautiful, are they not? Take them, feel the flesh, so soft, so round, so warm. Am I not a beautiful woman? Wouldn't it be wonderful to have me here in your arms in your office? It's so naughty and so dirty. I will pleasure you however you want," Linda spoke to me in an unworldly seductive tone. It was an extremely intense moment. I felt a number of simultaneous emotions—shock, attraction, fear, lust, and guilt—but I knew I couldn't surrender to Linda's advances. If she were nothing more than a lecherous woman, my professional ethics were at stake, and if she was in fact the victim of some demonic possession, I knew there was a lot more at stake than my reputation. I admit it was difficult to resist. Her eyes took on a hypnotic stare and I felt attracted like never before. There was something very distinctive in this seduction that I couldn't put my finger on. It was a real encounter for sure, but it almost felt as though I was in a dream or a trance. A hypnotic state perhaps, but it was tinged with something else. All at once I was lost in her eyes but I could at the very same instant see her exposed breasts, smell her perfume—and the strangest thing of all was that I felt as though we were having sex despite the fact that I had not even touched her! I was able to summon enough mental strength to gently push her away and explain that I felt what she was doing was out of line. I also realized that if Linda was in fact a succubus, then this was the moment when I could actually address the entity within. When demons are doing their work, their defenses are down and can be seen for what they truly are. It's at this moment when they can be vulnerable to a counterspell or at the very least be called out as to their true intentions. Although I wasn't prepared for any type of confrontation no less an exorcism, I could at least discover what I was up against.

Linda's breath was more labored by now, but she hadn't abandoned her attempted seduction. As much as I wanted to believe that her condition was nothing more than a normal, albeit hyper, sexual drive or some psychological malady or call for help, I sensed a presence in her and now within my office as well that was making me feel anxious and unclean. It was more than the promise of illicit sex. I knew that this was the right time to press Linda on who, or *what* she really was, so I began to play along with the seductive game. I said that we should talk more about what she wanted and the pleasures she had mentioned. I felt that if she could let her guard down, I could penetrate to the real truth. Although it was still difficult to break away from her gaze, I realized that if I slowly glanced back and forth between her eyes the hypnotic effect wasn't as strong. Demons often use a person's own resistance as "power boosters" to strengthen themselves. The more someone struggles, the more energy is drained and the more vulnerable that person becomes.

I tried a little psychology and asked Linda to tell me who she thought she had become in an effort to provoke the entity: "You mentioned that you have changed and you enjoy this new person you've become. Who is this person? Isn't it just still you with a new outlook on sex and pleasure? Aren't your actions just an excuse to get out of a boring marriage? Aren't you playing out this little psychodrama so people will think that you've lost your mind so you'll be pitied instead of scorned?"

Linda sat down on the couch in my office and slowly leaned back to stretch her tall body. Her skirt was now hiked well up past her knees as she languished on the sofa. Waiting for her response, I was surprised at how cool she was. There was no outburst of emotion or even a hint of annoyance. I at least expected her to be angered by my accusations. But I realized that if there were some otherworldly infestation, it would not have been affected by typically human comments. Why would a demon care if I accused its host of being a liar? And if Linda were really a succubus, she would have enjoyed the fact that I was headed down the wrong path. This made me take a different approach. I asked Linda to recall the particulars of the ritual and ceremony under the guise that I wanted to experience her newfound pleasures. I was playing along with the seduction so I could uncover the occult truth.

She explained to me that the ritual was a grand enlighten-
ment that opened all of her senses to the lustful beauty of life.
She said her eyes had become open to what is truly humanity's purpose on earth—to experience pleasure at all costs with
no regard for death. I asked how she knew these things and
she said they were made clear during the ritual. "The angels
had come and explained that the only way to live eternally
was to mate with them because they are the only true ethereal
beings that do not decay to dust," Linda said.

"But you are mating with anyone whom you can find.
They are men, not angels," I said.

Linda at first didn't respond. She then said that she only
used men to gain their power for herself. She seemed agitated
that she had let me in on this secret.

I surmised that this could be the succubus's M.O.—to har-
vest the essence of human semen. I felt as though I might
finally be getting a rise out of her, so I pressed onward. "You
didn't see angels in your ritual did you? They were just your
imagination. Or maybe just men you lust after."

"I mated with the beasts who are above men," Linda said.

This was another clue. Occult lore speaks of incubi man-
ifesting themselves as animals during erotic dreams. The
winged being in Linda's dream could have been an incubus in
a birdlike form. I knew I was onto something here, so I continued to probe Linda's memory of her ritual. I kept denying
the reality of her "angels" and said that her ritual was nothing
more than her imagination.

Linda began to squirm on the couch and then sat up. "It
was no sham. I have been in contact with beings you could
never imagine," she said.

"Okay, then name them. Tell me who they are. If you're
not playing some game, let me know who these angels are so

I can also summon them and take part in your revelation," I said.

Linda turned away from me and gazed out of the window. The lights from the office buildings across the street framed her silhouette and gave an eerie glow to her face as she turned her head to answer me. She looked me straight in the eye and began masturbating, over the outside of her clothes. Roger had told me before that Linda had taken to not wearing underwear since she began her new life and that she often exposed her private parts to men in public places—mostly in bars and restaurants. "I have been with he who has lived for eons. I am the harlot of Mahazael," Linda said. I was floored, and that was enough. I asked Linda to leave my office.

The next day I researched the name of Mahazael and as I suspected it is the ancient name of the demonic equivalent of the elemental angel of the earth who often appeared to sorcerers as a giant black condor. If Linda's ritual actually worked and if she had summoned the demon Mahazael, there was the fantastic possibility that she had become a living succubus bent on stealing the reproductive energies of every person she had sex with. I was, of course, skeptical that someone so new to the occult world could have ever been adept enough to perform a master ritual so successfully that she was able to summon a major demon. And it was a very long shot that Linda would know the name of Mahazael, since she was only a novice student of magic. I requested that Roger bring me all of the occult books and materials in Linda's possession so I could check her sources. I had found no mention of the demon Mahazael in any of Linda's dozen or so books, including the ritual book found in the walls of the old Magickal

Childe store. Unless Linda had another occult source, I was at a loss to know how she would know of Mahazael.

Epilogue

I returned the books to Roger about a week later and explained that I had found no trace of information explaining how Linda could know so much ancient esoteric lore. I also told him that barring any psychological abnormalities that I was obviously unqualified to diagnose, Linda appeared to have been strongly affected by some condition or some *thing* that caused her to be a sexual predator. He told me that she wasn't improving and in fact was becoming more and more obsessed with sex and that he was contemplating leaving her.

"She's still considering becoming a porn actress. She's got a stage name for herself and everything. She's calling herself 'Lili deLust'," Roger reluctantly said. In light of his troubles, I didn't mention to Roger that although most people know of "Lilith" as the archetypal female demon of history, most *don't know* that the early Assyrian insatiable female demon of lust who roamed the night looking for men to prey on and who was the inspiration for the Hebrew Lilith was actually named "Lili." Most are not aware of that bit of information—except maybe for Linda that is.

8.

The Salem Witch Connection

Silvana was well aware that X-Investigations never mixed business with pleasure. We had an agreement since we began the paranormal investigative team with Vincent's detective firm that we would not take on friends' or relatives' cases no matter how much they begged for our help. We knew from past experience that the second we would advise on a paranormal matter and even hint that the "victim" may have some psychological or personality problem, all hell would break loose and our relationship would quickly be in jeopardy. But Silvana always knew how to manipulate my weaknesses. She'd pout and slink around the room suggestively or hold on to my arm and tilt her head just enough to have to look up to me with her huge brown eyes.

I knew trouble was brewing one day when she started to circle my desk in that familiar catlike prowl, so I cut her short. "What is it, Silvana? What bizarre request are you poising yourself to hit me with?" I asked.

"Why, Robert, what makes you think I'm doing that? I'm simply a little bored and I think we should take a trip out of the city, that's all," she answered.

"Bored? We have piles of case material that must be filed into the computer and crosschecked with other paranormal and occult databases. It will take us weeks to get this stuff in order. How can you be bored?"

Silvana played the "I want to go on an adventure" game, which meant that she needed to tell me something very important but was a little afraid of how I'd react. After I ignored her for about fifteen minutes, she suddenly broke down and blurted out, "Robert, I have a friend who needs our help badly. He has been to a strange place and he has had contact with a coven of witches and an old murderous house and he has had many problems and he does not know what to do and. . . ."

"Hold on, hold on," I said. I was about to give her the company line about not getting involved with friends and relatives when I saw tears welling up in her eyes. Silvana had been the sheepish coquette before and won me over, but it was always a little game. This time she looked genuinely concerned and upset. I asked her to come out for a coffee and to discuss what was bothering her and her friend.

It started to rain heavily as we left our building on Second Avenue and raced to the coffee shop on the corner a block away. I hoisted my raincoat up over both of our heads and pulled Silvana's arm along to keep pace with me as we ran and jumped the quickly filling puddles that are Manhattan potholes. We sat in a booth near the window watching the unfortunate New Yorkers without umbrellas racing for cover or the more amusing few who were trying to hail a cab.

"So what's the problem? Who is this person and what

kind of mess is he into?" I asked. Silvana lowered her head and explained that she had met Mario in her citizenship class some years ago. He was an Italian immigrant and they had become close friends once they found that they had a common interest in the occult. Mario was fascinated with Silvana's keen perceptive "abilities," and Silvana was mesmerized by Mario's seemingly endless stories of Italian witchcraft and curses known as the *stregas*. Although Silvana had also emigrated from Europe, hers and Mario's cultures were very different, and they constantly compared notes about each other's paranormal and occult myths and folklore. Silvana said she would recall the vampire legends so common in her region and Mario would counter with the tales of the *mezza-omo*, or half-man specter that would float into the village homes in search of infants to steal for demonic rituals. If anyone looked at the mezza-omo face to face, the whole family would be cursed and the child would be taken. "Mario told me that one of his aunts saw the monster and her hair immediately turned completely gray," Silvana said.

I was almost ready to say to Silvana that it sounded like Mario had quite an imagination and that whatever "problem" he may have had was probably a result of an overactive fantasy and not a paranormal event. I also wanted to remind her that as paranormal investigators we had experienced a number of cases that turned out to be nothing more than the fabrications of bored people who told us all manner of "spooky" tales and unexplained events simply to stir up a little excitement in their otherwise mundane lives. We didn't have the time or the budget for wild goose chases, so we needed to be certain that whatever we investigated warranted our services. And to add to the problem, our benefactor, Vincent, often rolled his eyes when we returned from a case with either no payment or no concrete results. "This ain't no *Ghostbusters* movie we're doing here. This office space, phones, travel—everything costs money," he'd say. So I tried once again to impress on Silvana that whatever Mario's problem was, it had better be worth our efforts to solve it.

But she was ready for me. She mentioned two things that she knew would get my attention and most likely persuade me to take on the case: Salem, Massachusetts, and the old Joshua Ward House and book company in the center of that town.

Being no stranger to Salem, a favorite old "haunt" of mine if you will, I was delighted with the idea of returning to the "city of witches" to see old friends. Despite the overhyped tourism that unendingly touts Salem's notorious history as the center of witchcraft and the witch trials purported to end in burnings at the stake, many practicing Wiccans and numerous magickal organizations have settled in the New England city. What's more, I've always detected a certain genuine vibe of the mysterious and occult whenever I visited. Silvana had also felt Salem's odd attraction during previous cases and even on pleasure trips. If you love Halloween, as I do, Salem's the place to go during that holiday. It's almost Halloween all year round, and I always welcome a chance to visit.

What had happened to Mario in the New England town and how the Ward House figured into it was intriguing. The legend of the Ward House is steeped in murder and ghosts. The place is supposed to have been built on the site of the home of a crazed high sheriff, Giles Corey, who in the late seventeenth century was responsible for many of Salem's witch trials. The legend tells that the sheriff was so reviled in the community that his family buried him in the cellar of the house to prevent his body from being desecrated. Salem legend also tells of a man suspected of witchcraft who the sheriff crushed to death with stones. This fellow reportedly cursed the magistrate to haunt the grounds as an earthbound spirit for eternity. Numerous ghostly sightings have been reported at the Ward House in all areas of the building. Reports of a twisted-necked woman "floating" on the front stairs who intentionally frightens visitors away have been documented, as has the sighting of a dark outline of a disheveled and bearded old man who can be seen in the window—even from the street during broad daylight. I myself visited there one afternoon some years ago and I sensed an extremely eerie and malevolent feeling surrounding the house. But being so inclined— spooked and fascinated all at once—I never missed a chance to go back to see whether I could discover anyone or any "thing" new about the infamous house and grounds.

I finally gave in to Silvana and asked for the particulars about Mario and what she wanted us to do. She said she could tell me his story but she thought it would be better if we met with Mario so that he could explain the misfortunes that had resulted from his Salem encounter. "Robert, I can tell you the bad things. You know I have told you many times before bad things that we should fix, but my friend is very, very in trouble in his mind because of the curse and the ghosts," Silvana said.

"The curse? The ghosts!?" I asked "When were you going to tell me about these curses and ghosts? Maybe if you would have mentioned them from the beginning we could have saved a lot of time," I said snidely. The truth was that by this time I was hooked. Just the thought of revisiting Salem was appealing, and even if Mario's problem didn't warrant our time or effort, the mere thought of a new case involving the Ward House was enough. There have been numerous ghost hunting expeditions and some fairly convincing results, but we had never had the opportunity to get X-Investigations' contribution about the Ward House recognized in the world of paranormal research; this was the chance I'd been waiting for.

The House

Mario was not a nut, despite my preconception that he was probably a nervous type with New Age leanings and crystal pendants hanging from his neck. He was anything but odd-looking. When Silvana introduced us at her apartment a few nights later, I was happy to see that the gregarious Mario, a swarthy young man in his mid-thirties, appeared to be quite stable. He joked from the get-go about us being crazy ghost busters and how all good teams needed balance—me being the brains and Silvana being the beauty. Of course, Silvana chimed in and reminded Mario that *she* was in fact the one who had managed to get him through their immigration exams and that her contribution to the X-Investigations team was a lot more than pulchritude.

"Ah yes, but that's just my Italian charm showing through to you, Bella Silvana," Mario said.

Mario's jovial attitude quickly changed when I asked him what had happened in Salem and why it was so necessary to involve us. His face took on a pained expression as he put down his glass of wine to begin his story. As he looked at Silvana, she took his hand and told him that he could feel comfortable telling us everything. "We have heard and seen many strange things, Mario. You came to me for help because you trust me, and we will help you. But you must tell us everything—every detail—so we are prepared for whatever we may encounter," Silvana said.

Mario then relaxed and told us how his ordeal had begun. He was convinced by a girl he had met at a Learning Center Annex seminar that they should take a drive up to Salem one weekend to explore the town. Mario said Julie was very much into astrology and tarot cards, and she told him about Wiccan practices. Although she didn't consider herself a witch, she was curious and had read many books on the subject. Julie had always wanted to visit Salem and when she heard Mario's homeland stories of Italian witches (stregas) and occult beliefs, she convinced him that they would be perfect travel buddies for a jaunt up to "witch central." "I thought it would be lots of fun, and she was very attractive, so I figured what the hell?" Mario told us.

The trip started out normally enough. The new friends stayed at the Salem Inn, central to the town's tourist trade, and began to explore their surroundings. Julie was in her glory visiting the Witch's Museum, the Crow Haven Corner occult shop, and the many other not-so-genuine "spooky" stores that profit from Salem's infamous history. Julie was absorbing all she could of the local lore, specifics of Wiccan ritual, spells, and stories of luminaries like Laurie Cabot. The couple took an evening ghost tour of the town's cemeteries and haunted houses. Mario said that one of the women on the tour, a middle-aged woman with long, silver-gray hair, who happened to be a local resident, took an immediate liking to Julie, discussing Salem, witchcraft, and how most visitors only see the surface of Salem's deep occult roots. According to Mario, Julie was mesmerized by the woman, seemingly forgetting that Mario was even with her. Throughout the tour, this mysterious woman appeared to be more concerned with telling Julie about her local coven and the ancient and secret rituals the group performed, than with the tour at hand. She told Julie that at this time of the year during the Summer Solstice the group was particularly powerful and could perform astounding spell casting, the likes of which most people could never imagine. Mario admitted to us that he was annoyed that Julie had ignored him the minute a "real Salem witch" got her attention.

"I wanted to get Julie's attention back, so I interrupted their conversation and started talking about the Italian witches. Julie had heard some of these stories but not the more serious ones—like when the stregas give the evil-eye curse that is the most powerful curse in the world," Mario said. "I told the gray-haired witch on the tour that the Italian witches had practiced hundreds of years before any witch had come to Salem. I knew I'd made the lady mad, but I was upset myself."

By this time, the ghost tour had made its way to the Joshua Ward House, where Mario said his problems began. The group stood across the road from the house in order to get a perspective of the land on which it was located. As the tour guide was telling the story of the infamous sheriff and how he had been responsible for the hanging of many suspected Salem witches, Mario said he had made a comment under his breath about the gray-haired woman stealing Julie's attention. He said that when the tour guide noted that many witches had met their fate at the gallows, he couldn't control what leapt from his mouth. "I said that the sheriff must have missed one witch, because she was standing right next to me here. I guess

I made the comment because I was mad at her for butting into my nice weekend with Julie," Mario admitted. He said that the stranger quickly shot a cold glance at him with "shiny black eyes" that sent chills up his spine. As the tour guide moved the group closer to the house, the older woman said to Julie that perhaps she would like to visit one of her coven's ceremonies that were taking place that very weekend. Julie jumped at the invitation, and then finally acknowledged Mario's presence, taking his hand as they crossed the street to get closer to the Joshua Ward House. Julie, Mario, and their new acquaintance, who never revealed her name, were at the back of the group and as the guide gave her talk, the gray-haired witch suggested that the three of them go to the back of the house because that's where many of the sightings had been recorded and it was supposedly over the exact spot where the sheriff's body had been buried.

The three sneaked away from the group and quietly made their way to the back of the house across a dark driveway littered with leaves. Mario said that the older woman was acting strange, positioning herself in front of Julie as they walked to the back of the house. Once they got to a particular spot that seemed familiar to the gray-haired witch, she moved Julie to her left side, saying that that was where she would get the best view. At the same time, she suspiciously maneuvered Mario to a spot about two feet behind the women and facing the back of the house at a 90-degree angle. "You can get the best view from here of the shape of the sheriff's ghost," the old witch said to Julie. When Mario asked why she had placed him in such an odd spot, the woman said that she had advised people many times before and that if he wanted to see things other people hadn't he shouldn't question her motives. Mario decided that he had already caused enough friction, so he decided to be quiet and play along.

"Then this crazy woman closed her eyes and started some kind of weird chanting in a very low voice. Julie thought this was very cool and she smiled at me while we watched as the woman threw her head back, stretched out her arms with her palms upward, and kept on chanting," Mario said. He told us that he was getting very spooked by the woman's actions and he wanted to get Julie away from her. He said that although they were not far from the group, they felt as if they were being pushed farther and farther away. As the woman continued chanting, they became more aware that they were somehow being transported—not to another place, but to another time. Mario described the sensation: "It felt like one of the crazy movies like when you see time moving really, really fast in a blur and you see seasons change in front of your eyes, or flowers grow and then die all in a split second." Silvana and I acknowledged each other's glance. We had both been witness to other cases where clients similarly described out-of-body experiences like Mario's, but they were always self-generated. Based on what Mario had told us, the woman had either hypnotized the couple or produced some kind of spell that created a feeling of time change.

I asked Mario where he had felt he was at that precise moment. He said that he wasn't sure whether he had fallen asleep and was dreaming or if he was actually in another time. But he thought his surroundings looked look quite different from the back area of the house when he and Julie had first walked to the back. "I cannot explain it too well, but we were not in the same place when that happened to us. That witch did something to me and Julie," Mario said.

The case assumed some paranormal merit at this point. When Mario excused himself to use the bathroom, I told Silvana that the case sounded interesting but not solid enough to justify devoting a lot of our time. When Mario returned, I told him that his experience could be explained in a number of ways—maybe the witch slipped him some sort of hallucinogenic "mickey", or perhaps it had been a hysterical reaction to the overwhelming Salem sense of the occult. "It's rare, but not impossible, that you and Julie would both have the same experience. But you haven't told us enough to warrant conducting a serious investigation," I said.

"But that was just the beginning, Robert. I didn't tell you what we saw and what has been happening ever since. This is the real problem, not just that moment. It's the ghost of the sheriff that is ruining my life," Mario continued.

On the short plane ride from New York to Logan International Airport in Boston, I went over the particulars of the case with Silvana. During the odd time-shift Mario had experienced at the back of the Joshua Ward House, he claimed that he had actually seen some kind of ethereal being racing across the grounds where he stood frozen. The being had slammed an axe through the back door and then run screaming through the house. The ghostly apparition then settled in a window of the house and grinned at Mario, as if to indicate that he would be his next victim. Mario had been transfixed by the image and could sense pure evil, as it stared him in the eye from behind the panes of glass. He described the face as being wrinkled and "twisted with evil," with a gray-yellow pallor. The gray-haired witch was laughing and cackling frantically as though she was a deranged puppeteer pulling the specter's strings. What seemed to Mario like nearly a half-hour had actually lasted only a few minutes, according to his wristwatch. When it was over, he felt extremely tired, as though he hadn't slept for days. Once he cleared his senses, Mario had had a serious argument with the gray-haired witch over Julie leaving the tour group to join the coven in a ritual it planned for midnight that evening. Mario was not invited, but the older woman was adamant that Julie join them despite his strong objections.

As their argument grew more heated, the witch told Mario that what they had experienced at the back of the Ward House was the result of a spell she had cast to demonstrate her power to Julie. The woman said that her coven, an ancient sect of Celtic Wiccans whose ancestors had settled in Salem in the 1600s, had an intense magical hold on the area and could control the powers of this world and the next to do their bidding. It appeared as though Julie had been chosen to be a new recruit and that Mario just happened to be an unwanted bystander who was standing in her way. Mario later learned that the spell the woman had cast was not performed simply to impress Julie but in fact had a more malevolent purpose—to conjure the ghost of Salem's infamous high sheriff to do her bidding. Mario told us that according to the witch, during the witch trials when the sheriff had condemned one of the coven's ancestors to death, the accused witch cursed the sheriff and bound his spirit to answer to the wishes of her generations to come for all eternity. Mario feared that because he and the gray-haired woman had argued so vehemently about allowing Julie to attend the midnight ceremony, she might be angry enough to make him the target of the sheriff's ghost.

Silvana shuffled through our notes and read off a list of problems that Mario had faced since his return from Salem. We needed to address these one by one in order to determine which obstacles might actually be the result of paranormal influence. The list contained the following:

1. Experienced recurring, bizarre, extremely vivid dreams centering on Salem. The dreams always depicted screaming people, fire, black-walled enclosures, and frantic running from house to house

2. Noticed that missing items from Mario's apartment all were somehow connected to his trip to Salem

3. Strange odors of earth and sea on Mario's person and clothing

4. Flashes of wispy light and orbs of light streaking through his apartment

5. Stopped from visiting Julie at her home on three different occasions because of car trouble, weather, and sickness

Mario had the most intense and disturbing experience the second night after his return from Salem. He arrived at his apartment at about 11:45 after a date with Julie. It had been a rather unpleasant evening; Julie had berated him for arguing with the gray-haired woman on the ghost tour. He decided to try to let it go and to get a good night's sleep. But that wasn't to be so easy. He had fallen asleep quickly enough, but it was a labored sleep—he had been twisting and turning and feeling very cold despite being bundled under the blankets. When he awoke from his restlessness, he noticed the distinct smell of sea air in his pitch-dark room. He sat up frantically, searching for the switch on his bedside lamp. If he looked toward the corner window of his bedroom, Mario knew he could see a glimmer of street light to guide him, but he realized in sudden horror that he could not open his eyes! No matter how hard he tried, he could not raise his eyelids. He was blind in the pitch dark and the normal brain control mechanism that opened his eyes thousands of times a day was not working. He was powerless to see. He grabbed at his eyes with his fingers, trying to pry open the lids, but he could not budge them. He put one hand on the top of his eyes and the other below and stretched his skin so his eyes would open, but despite tiny tears in the corners of his eyes he still could not get them open. He could feel blood trickle down his fingers from where he had stretched the skin around his eyes to the breaking point and he hoped the lubrication might help them open, but his eyes remained shut. Exhausted and frightened, he laid back in bed and then heard a sickening laugh ringing in his ears: "Pray for death, your hell is here on earth."

He could not explain what happened next other than to say that he had fallen asleep again. He awoke the next morning, sight restored, in sweat-dried sheets. This bizarre event caused Mario to become obsessed with the legend of the high sheriff in an effort to rid himself of his haunting. He had done hours of research on the Web, but despite the volume of information he compiled on his computer's hard drive and the hundreds of pages of printouts of everything he found, every bit of information had somehow been lost, misplaced, or accidentally destroyed.

We always approach a case as skeptics and one of our first methods is to try to determine if odd events are anything more than mere coincidence. So, before we left on our investigation to Salem, we scrutinized Mario's claims and even conducted our own "acid test." We found a complimentary postcard from the Salem Inn stashed in his suitcase. We asked him to identify the postcard, which he did without suspicion.

Without telling Mario, we then hid the postcard behind a picture on the wall. On a later visit the postcard was gone. Of course, we asked Mario if he had found it while cleaning, and he said he hadn't. He said that he was wondering about the postcard's whereabouts because he wanted to send it to relatives back in Italy. This was a minor test, but it corroborated Mario's claims and fit with the mysterious events surrounding Mario's dilemma.

The Discovery

During our drive from Logan to Salem, Silvana admitted to me that she had never visited the town, not so much because she never had the opportunity but more because she had heard that there were many disturbed spirits in the area and her precognitive abilities often warned her to stay away. It was obvious that Silvana was becoming antsy in the rental car as she revealed her uneasiness about Salem. She repeatedly mentioned that Mario's problem was probably not a paranormal event at all, probably in a half-hearted attempt to quell her apprehension. I asked her if she would rather not go into town, but she insisted that although she felt some ominous warnings, her job—*our* job—was to flush out the cause of Mario's disturbance. But Silvana's instincts were always on the money, so I knew that if she was that spooked, then we were in for a case for the books. I was all at once jazzed that we had a real event on the hook, while at the same time worried that we could be messing with powers much stronger than we had yet experienced. Our first stop in Salem was Crow Haven Corner to try to find the gray-haired witch.

Although Laurie Cabot no longer owned the shop that sits on the corner adjacent to the town commons and across from the tourist-heavy Witch Museum, I was able to locate Lance, a long-time employee and student of the paranormal who had helped me with information for a number of other cases in the New England area. It wasn't long before we dug up the person we sought—her name was Jazael, the high priestess of a Dianic Wiccan coven that operated on the outskirts of Salem proper. Unlike almost any other town in America, in Salem one can find a Wiccan high priestess faster than a local dentist. And with a local who's connected to the occult network, the results are immediate.

We had lunch with Lance in a local pub and I felt glad to be in Salem again, even under these circumstances. I was also glad that Lance and Silvana had connected on some psychic level because she was beginning to feel more comfortable about being in the area. Lance told us that although Jazael was well known in town most people didn't know any real details about her other than that her family had been original Salem settlers and her coven members did not speak of her to anyone in town. The Dianic coven that Jazael ruled was for women only, and it was rumored to be a lesbian sect. But what made us really take notice was what Lance revealed just before biting into his tuna sandwich: Jazael's sect recruited *only* Salem natives or those whose ancestors could be directly traced to the town.

Our call to Vincent's office that afternoon confirmed what we had suspected. Thanks to the speed of the Internet and Vincent's detective database, a trace of Julie's family history did indeed lead straight to Salem—something that Julie herself probably didn't know. Her family had been early settlers well documented in Massachusetts's records as bookbinders.

There was, however, one black mark on the family record that appeared to be more of a missing item than a formal note. A member of Julie's family had some difficulties with the local magistrate in 1658, but the details were suspiciously omitted. The computer report simply read: "The true confession has purged the offense." It is common knowledge that during the witch hunts of that era if a person was accused of being a witch and confessed, she was usually released . . . as long as she was willing to give details about other known witches and their ceremonies. This, of course, begged the question of whether Julie's ancestor was a witch "stoolie," or if we were making a bad assumption. But what we did know was that Jazael had discovered Julie's past by some unknown (occult?) means.

I now ruled out any coincidence in this matter because the entire case was weaving together too perfectly. Jazael wanted Julie as part of her coven, and Mario was in the way during the ghost tour and was continuing to see Julie. But Silvana reminded me of the Joshua Ward House and questioned how or why that was a piece of the strange puzzle. The obvious connection was the ghost of the high sheriff. If Jazael could in fact control the spirit through her spell castings and let it loose on Mario, that could explain his current problems. It was becoming clear that a ghost bound to the Salem witch sect was haunting Mario. Now all that we had to do was have Jazael remove the spell and set Mario free. But first we had to be convinced that the ghost was *real*.

Lance, our Salem operative, managed to arrange a meeting for us with Jazael under the guise that we were New York television producers willing to pay big money for an on-air interview with a real witch. Although those in the occult take their practices very seriously, money still has its own special powers in the material world.

We began asking very general questions about Wicca and Salem and then moved into the witch trials and the ghost of the high sheriff. Jazael's calm demeanor became a bit ruffled when we mentioned that we heard of a legend that claimed because of the sheriff's heinous crimes against witches and suspected witches his spirit was magically bound by a local coven. She said that there are many strange things in Salem and those who are that curious need to discover the proof for themselves. "I cannot confirm nor deny that we as witches have hold over ethereal beings. Let's just say it's our little secret," Jazael said. I then asked her if she knew of occult lore that said if a witch's curse is made known, she must admit it to the inquisitor and give the details.

She said that was aware of such a method, at which time Silvana broke in and challenged Jazael, "We know you are trying to make Julie a member of your coven and you have used the high sheriff's ghost to make trouble for Julie's boyfriend, Mario." She then went on to describe Mario's recounting of the ghost tour spell and how he felt he was suspended in time and how he saw a crazed entity running through the Joshua Ward House.

Silvana's sudden burst of enthusiasm surprised me, but I was glad that we ended the charade so quickly. Jazael turned her head and said that she had the power to curse and that we should believe what we wanted. But she warned us not to interfere—we wouldn't want to get in the way of a loosed spirit known to be a murderer. I reminded Jazael that there are many powerful magicians in the world, and also reminded her of the witches' rede that states "An' it harm none, do what thou wilt." If she were bent on doing harm to Mario in a selfish effort to gain a new member of her coven, there would be a price to pay down the line.

We had hoped that this encounter would convince Jazael to call off her ghost, if in fact she was the catalyst for Mario's problems. We called him at his apartment the next morning and told him of what we learned and our confrontation with Jazael and about Julie's family tree. We were happy to hear that although his hauntings had been chronic, since last evening he hadn't experienced any weird occurrences. The timing curiously coincided with our talks with Jazael—and this made us hopeful that perhaps she had lifted whatever spell she might have cast on Silvana's friend. But as good as everything sounded, I remained curious about the happenings at the Joshua Ward House. After all, it has been a hotbed of rumor, legend, and ghostly activity for years. I convinced Silvana that we should take a ride to the house before we made our way back to New York.

It was about 4:00 P.M. when we finally settled our bill at the Hawthorne Hotel at the Salem Commons and drove the short distance to the Ward House. Silvana said to me, "So this is the famous spooky house, eh? It doesn't look so scary to me. It is a nice brick building with nice window drapes." I had to agree, it didn't look very ominous in the afternoon light and I was also a little disappointed by its rather tame presence. I didn't feel particularly creepy and Silvana's psychic sensitivity wasn't sounding any alarms.

So I took out my Nikon camera and began snapping some photos for posterity's sake and also to keep in Mario's file. I shot some photos of the front of the house and the signage, and then I remembered that Mario's event had taken place at the back of the house. We ventured back there to shoot a few stills. It looked peaceful enough, and I was confident that this case could be put to bed.

Epilogue

A week later I telephoned Mario to check in and he happily said everything seemed to be back to normal. He was still seeing Julie and her obsession with Salem appeared to have been overshadowed by a new interest in yoga. I mentioned to him that we theorized that the ghost of the high sheriff might have been the poltergeist that was playing havoc with his life and we hoped that our talk with Jazael had convinced her to back off. "So she was really a witch who cursed me because I like Julie?" Mario asked. I told him that it looked that way, especially considering how things were settling down after our confrontation with Jazael. As I hung up, Silvana walked into the office and handed me the package of photos from One Hour Photo that I had taken of the Joshua Ward House. I quickly shuffled though the pictures, which also included shots of the Salem town square and various points of interest. The Ward House photos were at the back of the pack and I nearly dropped them on the floor when I saw the results. Two of the pictures contained ghostly wisps of light that streaked around the house. One photo showed an ominous specter standing in the window. I asked Silvana to take a look at what I believed to be spirits caught on film and she said, "Ah, the high sheriff is back where he belongs."

9.

The Cats Made
Her Kill Herself

It was one of the most somber calls we had ever received at X-Investigations. A cold-call client, Alexis, told Silvana that her great aunt, Phyllis, whom she had loved as a mother since she was a child, had recently taken her own life. The sixty-eight-year-old woman was not sick, depressed, or financially troubled—typical reasons for someone to commit suicide. But the police had deemed the death a suicide, so that's the way the record read. Alexis sounded teary on the phone, so Silvana listened intently out of respect for the girl's grief, but she was wondering why she was calling the paranormal arm of Vincent's detective agency. X-Investigations had a separate phone number, so Silvana thought perhaps Alexis somehow confused the numbers and was seeking our partner organization. Whatever the reason, Silvana was immediately taken by the girl's story. Alexis said she really didn't believe that Phyllis would do such a thing. "She was always very happy and she loved hearing from me. There was nothing in the world that would have caused her to do such a terrible thing to herself. My aunt would never kill herself, it's just too bizarre to believe," Alexis said.

Alexis went on to explain that Phyllis had lived alone in her Westchester, New York, home since the death of her husband, Arnold, about two years before and didn't really want for anything. Arnold had been a bank executive who had done very well in the stock market and had left his wife well off.

Silvana interrupted Alexis to ask, "Do you have a problem that you need a detective to investigate for you concerning your aunt's death?"

"A detective? Oh, no. I am calling X-Investigations, am I not?" Alexis responded.

Silvana answered in the affirmative and slowly explained that we handle cases that are not "usual" and that deal with the occult and paranormal. Alexis said, "Oh, yes, I know, that's why I called. You see, I know my aunt didn't kill herself. It was the cats . . . her evil cats. They're the ones that killed Aunt Phyllis. They made it look like she did it to herself but they were the cause. I'm sure of it. It was the evil cats. They're all black, you know, and I told Aunt Phyllis for many years that black cats were evil but she told me I was superstitious and that the cats were really magical and not evil at all."

Despite Silvana's special psychic abilities and her usually reliable character assessments, she felt that Alexis's plea had some basis in fact and she listened closely to the cat story. She knew that if she presented the problem as a possible case for us, she better have good reason.

My nut meter went off immediately when Silvana finally told me the details of Alexis's phone call. We're used to having every kind of crazy asking us for help with the most bizarre circumstances imaginable, but sometimes calls are so out there that my common sense tells me that pursuing them would be nothing more than a waste of time. This seemed like one of those. "Cats?! Black cats that caused an elderly woman to kill herself? C'mon, Silvana, you know we don't have time for these kinds of nut ball claims. Plus, you said yourself that the girl told you the police closed the case as a suicide, which means we'd have to get the coroner's records, police reports, and whatnot just to get the details. And more important, where's the occult angle? What's so paranormal about the case? Did Alexis give you a hint as to why she thought the cats made the old lady kill herself, or is there some kind of inheritance deal going on here? Maybe she got aced out of some money so she wants people to think the old gal was loony so they could reopen the case and her will," I said.

Silvana and I discussed the merit of the case at the end of the day while straightening out some long overdue filing. "But, Robert, the girl sounded so troubled and sincere. I feel that there may be something to her story. She told me her aunt's stories about the cats and that her aunt was becoming obsessed with what they wanted. She first gave them expensive food and did crazy things like buy them special beds and their own TVs!"

"So, that's not our problem. There are many, many people who spoil their pets and buy them all kinds of ridiculously expensive things. Look at all of the rich people's pets that we see on those lifestyle shows. I really don't see this warrants us to invest time in this case, Silvana," I answered.

But then Silvana mentioned the one piece of evidence that piqued my curiosity. During the phone call, Alexis had played a tape recording that put Silvana over the edge. Although Alexis admitted that her aunt was getting older and perhaps losing some of her mental faculties, when she told her niece that the cats actually spoke to her, Alexis had become truly alarmed. She told Silvana that Phyllis had spent many hours studying the history of cats' magical abilities, from ancient Egyptian culture through medieval times right up to the present. Phyllis had become a fanatical believer that cats not only possessed supernormal abilities, but were also endowed with spiritual powers and were nothing short of godlike. She would rant for hours about how the cats spoke to her in many different languages and told her of the secrets of the universe and how humans are the inferior species on earth. She said the cats had instructed her in the preparation of potions and formulas for invisibility, flying, and shape-shifting. And the elderly woman had proof! She had notebooks filled with recipes and formulas that she would show Alexis whenever her niece visited for afternoon tea. To Alexis's amazement, the instructions were meticulously detailed, containing exotic herbs and odd ingredients like nightshade and snakeskin, and the accompanying ceremonies were in many languages— mostly Latin and a strange language called "Enochian", which Alexis found out about after some Internet research.

Of course, Alexis discounted much of what her aunt compiled as the fantasies of a bored, lonely woman, and consoled herself by thinking her aunt could have simply copied the writings in her notebooks from library books or TV. But the one disturbing and eerie action that concerned Alexis most about her aunt's sanity and well-being were the tape-recorded conversations Phyllis claimed were between her and the cats. Just as Silvana was about to end the call, Alexis asked her to please listen to her aunt's recordings. She had found the microtapes along with notebooks in an old piece of leather luggage buried in her aunt's attic.

There were some sixty different tapes of about thirty minutes each, all labeled with strange titles like "To Make a Dream" and "From Human Body to Human Body." Some of the tapes were simply labeled "Conversation" and suffixed with a number. One, however, was labeled "Conversation with Tailspring" and had a star drawn next to it. Alexis explained that Tailspring was the name of one of her aunt's black cats, the "alpha cat" and leader of the nine household felines. "Uncle Arnold always complained about Tailspring, primarily because he was the first cat Aunt Phyllis brought into the house about ten years ago and also because he seemed to have a mind of his own despite what any human demanded. If Tailspring couldn't make his way out of the house at night to roam because the doors were shut or everyone was asleep, he would knock over lamps or dishes, inevitably breaking something of value. It was strange, but he never ruined anything insignificant, it was always something Aunt Phyllis loved or one of Uncle Arnold's prized model ships or airplanes. Even after Uncle Arnold put all of his models in a special case, Tailspring managed to shake the case against the wall during one of his tantrums about being trapped in the house, causing a model ship to fall and break. They finally installed a cat door in the back of the house—something Uncle Arnold hadn't wanted to do out of fear that rodents would enter, but he had begrudgingly capitulated. 'Damn it, Green Eyes (a pet name for my aunt), that cat's got to go!' he'd say, but he never enforced his demand. No, Uncle Arnold didn't like Tailspring very much and the more cats that Aunt Phyllis added to the brood, the more upset with them all he became," Alexis said.

Alexis convinced Silvana to listen to the tape labeled "Tailspring," which began innocently enough. Silvana said she could hear Phyllis introducing the conversation and speaking to the cats like any other pet lover would. She recorded the date for posterity and mentioned that Tailspring had something very important to reveal to the world. For the first five or six minutes Phyllis spoke about most peoples' misunderstanding of the true nature and purpose of cats. Silvana told me that there were some rather esoteric comments from Phyllis that one wouldn't expect to hear from an elderly woman, such as references to Madame Blavatsky (the founder of Theosophy, a pseudoreligion and philosophy grounded in the belief in superbeings who possessed secret wisdom and who inhabited the earth long before the emergence of humanity). In this tape's introduction, Phyllis noted that unknown to most of humanity, cats—all felines—are the direct descendants of the "secret beings" and will inherit the earth through what we erroneously describe as mystical means but that are in fact universal truths humanity is incapable of understanding. Background sound on the tape, as expected, featured a number of cats meowing and hissing. Silvana still wasn't sold on the validity of Alexis's claim or concern about what had happened to her aunt until Alexis asked her to listen intently to the next few seconds on the tape. Phyllis began to address the group of cats and Silvana noticed that oddly enough, the background cat noises suddenly stopped, as though a speaker at a seminar requested the gathering's attention. Phyllis announced, "Master Tailspring, we who are but flesh in inferior form ask your guidance. Please speak to us in the manner that we can comprehend, and we will do your bidding."

What followed blew Silvana away. Although the tape's quality was poor and sounded like Phyllis had moved the microphone away from the primary source, Silvana said she began to hear what sounded like a muffled human voice that was distinctly *not* Phyllis's. "I heard low conversation at first, like there were more people in the room than just Phyllis. I then realized that the voices started as cat meows and somehow they became voices, Robert. Like it would sound . . . *meow, meow, my name is* . . . like the cat started to talk. I know that this is crazy talk, but that is what I heard."

Once she heard this bizarre tape recording of Phyllis and her cats, or whatever or whoever else was in the room with her, Silvana's amazement at the circumstances convinced her to pitch the case to me. She figured that at the very least we could learn something from the tapes, even if they were doctored frauds. Many of our cases indeed concluded as nothing more than hoaxes or scams, and the more we knew about how paranormal hucksters did their jobs, the better we'd be at busting them. On the other hand, if we discovered a gem of a real unexplained event, then we'd be far ahead of the field—so it was academic for us to take Alexis's case.

The Mystical Cats

We made an appointment to meet Alexis at her aunt's house. Phyllis's will bequeathed the house to the cats, and whenever there's such a peculiar bequest, the legalities are challenged. This case was no exception. Because Alexis had inherited all of Phyllis's capital, the court decided that until the challenge to the cats was settled Alexis would be named the caretaker of the property. It was more than likely that the house would have to be sold, despite Phyllis's wishes that the cats remain in the house and someone be appointed to care for them. Phyllis noted in her will that the cats would decide who that person would be, but it wasn't quite clear how they were going to manage the choice other than that the nine black cats "would communicate their choice to the chosen person through a method that person would understand."

After Phyllis's death, the cats were taken in by a local shelter according to the will's instructions—all except Tailspring, who had suspiciously disappeared. Tailspring was a nocturnal wanderer but he always returned home by morning, according to Alexis. We accepted her gracious invitation to stay in the house as we conducted our investigation and so we could get a feel for Phyllis's total environment. It also gave us the opportunity to sharpen Silvana's psychic radar so that she could determine whether there was any ethereal residue of Phyllis that could give us a clue to the circumstances of her death.

When we entered the house, Silvana immediately told me that she knew there was a presence of vibrating energy nearby and she would pinpoint its location shortly. As Alexis and I spoke about the cats and where they were being held, Silvana zeroed in on the vibe. She took my hand and led me upstairs to Phyllis's bedroom—a neat, well-appointed room—just what one would expect from an elderly widow. It was a rather large room with dark maroon carpeting and Victorian-style furniture. The windows were draped in frilly white lace curtains that blocked out most of the hot southern sun. The only thing that was the least bit out of the ordinary was the number of photo frames in the room. Both night tables, Phyllis's dressing table and vanity, and a few wall shelves all displayed photos of the nine cats. Some single portraits and some of pairs or groups. What struck me about the photos more than the inordinate number was that each picture was perfectly posed, as though the animals were not real. Photos of pets are usually never so perfectly posed unless professionally done and then with very obedient pets. Most house pet photos I've seen feature the animals running, sleeping, or posing with humans. But not these. In each one, the cats looked directly at the photographer and sat still, almost as though they were paintings. Each cat, whether by itself or in a group, looked *directly* at the camera with a defiant, almost grinning facial expression. It was as though the cats knew something no one else knew—some secret they wouldn't share—and they were arrogantly smug about it. None of the photos included humans, not even Phyllis. I would have thought that a cat lover like her would have liked to have at least one picture of herself alongside her feline family, but there was no such picture.

As I focused on the photos, Silvana sat on the edge of the bed in preparation for meditation. After working a number of cases with Silvana, I knew all of her moves. When a feeling of some paranormal presence becomes overwhelming, she becomes intently aware and weakened by the sensory barrage. She closed her eyes and lowered her head into her hand ready to receive whatever "message" was being beamed into her brain. This was a strong vibration coming her way, so I sat down on the bed next to her and held her hand. Her eyes were closed and her head rolled from side to side as her body stiffened. She was squeezing my hand tightly and I could see beads of sweat break out above her full lips. Just at the point when I thought she would gyrate off the bed altogether, she became calm and opened her eyes. She looked toward the ceiling and pointed her index finger to the area by the closet door. "It is in the attic, Robert. The presence of the cats is up there behind the door," she said.

We called for Alexis and asked permission to open the closet. As we suspected, there was a panel in the ceiling of

Phyllis's bedroom that opened into the attic. We quickly pulled down the attic stairs to see what was causing Silvana's psychic disturbance. A cool breeze blew dust down into our faces as I climbed the stairs and yanked on the thin white string to turn on the single forty-watt bulb that lit the attic. Silvana said she could feel what we were looking for and that it was contained. Alexis entered the closet and called up to us that she had found her aunt's luggage with the notebooks and the tapes in the attic. "I was already up there and those things are all I found," she said.

But Silvana insisted that there was something else in the attic, something much more intense and disturbing than notebooks or tapes.

We searched the attic for the better part of an hour, turning over old furniture, looking in boxes of clothes, and flipping through magazines. Night was falling now and the attic was beginning to grow cold. I felt we had been searching aimlessly for far too long, although I respect Silvana's abilities. I was just about to call it quits for the night, when Silvana was suddenly quiet. I couldn't see her clearly in the dim light, so I called her name. Alexis got me a flashlight, which I shined in Silvana's direction. She was sitting in the far corner of the attic with her legs crossed yoga style, her upper torso completely erect and staring straight ahead. The flashlight beam illuminated the whites of her eyes and from my standpoint it looked as though Silvana's head was floating bodiless in the dark. She finally spoke, "Robert, I found what we were looking for." As the words came out of her mouth, both of her hands began to rise and I could see, even from twenty feet away, the yellow-white form of a complete cat skeleton.

Silvana had found the cat remains in a box wedged behind

two 2 × 4 wooden beams at the front of the attic. On inspection of the box, we couldn't find any evidence of a decomposed animal so we concluded that it hadn't died recently. We thought it had perhaps been buried and exhumed years later, or that Phyllis might have obtained the skeleton from some outside source. Why she had it and what it was doing in her attic was a mystery.

The discovery puzzled Alexis but interestingly did not seem to shock her. The revelation of the skeleton led us to the real reason that she suspected the animals had something to do with her aunt's death. She told us that her worries about the notebooks and recordings were only part of the bizarre story and that her aunt had rambled on about death and how her cats were going to transfer her soul so she could become one of the "secret masters" and join them as gods. "For quite a while after Uncle Arnold passed away, I simply humored Aunt Phyllis. She would go on and on about the cats, each time adding a new member to her 'family.' She said that she had to have a council of nine cats to complete the tasks that would help her truly understand the universal mysteries. And, of course, she would always talk about Tailspring, her favorite, whom she'd stroke on her lap and say that the two of them were joined in spirit and would never be apart. She would say, 'Alexis my dear, you must be aware of how felines have been magical creatures for eons. Just look at ancient Egypt and how they worshipped Bast, the cat-headed goddess. Even Leonardo da Vinci knew. He said the smallest feline is a masterpiece.'"

Alexis went on to tell us that Phyllis was quite the authority on the mysteries of cats, detailing to her that cats were so revered in ancient Egyptian culture that when a family cat died the household members shaved their eyebrows

and mourned the feline—some even embalmed and mummi-
fied their dead companions. She said she had an ominous feeling that Phyllis had been experimenting with mummification
in the event her cats should predecease her. As time went on,
Phyllis had begun exhibiting more bizarre behavior and telling
Alexis that the cats were not simply pets or companions, but
were in fact her spiritual guides. A religious person all of her
life, Phyllis had gradually turned away from her conventional
faith, telling Alexis that her cats were the ultimate answer to
life's mysteries and she would sacrifice everything and anything to join them in the total bliss of their paradise.

My natural response to Alexis's story was to ask if she
advised her aunt to seek some psychological help. "Oh, yes. I
was very discreet at first, telling her that she needed to talk to
someone after Uncle Arnold died and that she needed a close
human companion to fill the void. And she did see a therapist
for about six months. The therapist reported to me that Aunt
Phyllis was perfectly adjusted and could take care of herself
just fine."

"Was this before or after she started talking about mummification and the talking cats?" I asked.

"Well, it was before, but I did convince the therapist to
pay a visit at a later date, under the guise of having a friendly
chat after her bizarre behavior began, but he reported back to
me that she still seemed totally sane," Alexis said.

At this point, we decided to turn in for the night and continue our investigation the next day. We'd also take the cat
skeleton to our forensic specialist, Paula, to determine how
old the cat was. It was nearly 4:00 A.M. when I was awakened
out of a deep sleep by some clanging noises from the kitchen
downstairs. I cautiously headed down the stairs and peeked
over the banister to see who or what was in the kitchen. I

was happy to see Silvana's shapely outline by the sink. She was rinsing out a glass. My associate couldn't sleep and had decided to get a drink of juice. We pulled up a couple of chairs at the kitchen table and agreed that despite the fact that we'd spent nights in supposedly haunted houses and possessed establishments, it was rather strange to be in the ordinary person's home where we really didn't belong. "At least in a house that is haunted, we are there to be helpers. Here, we are not guests to help, but we are strangers. I don't feel the person has really left here yet, Robert. I still feel Phyllis's spirit is not gone," Silvana said in her best Czech psychic-talk.

I couldn't have agreed more. I thought maybe it was because the house still looked lived-in or because it was so ordinary, but that feeling of being an intruder was prevalent. I got up to refill my glass of juice, and I stopped dead in my tracks. I was glancing out the large kitchen window that looked into the dark backyard, when I noticed two huge green eyes staring at me. At first, I thought it was the reflection of something in the kitchen, perhaps a painting on the wall or a statue. On closer inspection, I realized that a huge black cat was sitting on the patio table, peering directly into the kitchen at Silvana and me. I called to her, but she had already seen the animal looking in at us.

"What the—where did she come from?" I asked Silvana.

In what seemed like an instant, it was gone. We opened the patio door to see if we could get another glimpse, but the cat was nowhere in sight. Silvana and I had the same question: Was this Tailspring returning home? If so, at least Alexis should know.

Our kitchen racket woke Alexis. Before we could summon her, she joined us in the kitchen. We told her what we saw and described the animal. From our description, Alexis deduced that it was in fact Tailspring returning home and said that it would be great if we confirm this. Then there would be no legal confusion regarding the challenge to the will.

"I don't want people to think that I deliberately got rid of Tailspring to void the will," Alexis said.

I grabbed the flashlight we used in the attic, telling Silvana and Alexis to follow me into the yard. Before I could open the patio door, we heard Tailspring howling a mournful meow. We couldn't see the cat, but we could hear a noise that sounded as though he was in terrible pain. It was a long, mournful cry that began as a typical meow and stretched into a loud howling that sounded like the name "Harold" drawn out into a two-syllable yodel. The bellow stopped us dead. And then things got worse.

The single cry from Tailspring or whatever other cat was in the yard suddenly multiplied into a duet of howling cats. The duet quickly turned into a battle of catcalls, one louder than the other, crying into the early dawn. The two cries turned into three, then four, and then more than we could count. Within minutes the entire yard was filled with what sounded like dozens, perhaps a hundred cats howling, screeching, crying, and moaning in a frightening, deafening, and eerie chorus. We expected to see cat fur flying everywhere. The distinct odor of cat urine in the air became a smothering stench. The putrid smell mixed with the meows created a surreal vortex, causing us to trip over each other in our hysterical race for cover. The cats were so loud the kitchen windows shook and the ceiling fan began to turn from the intense vibrations. We ran into the house and slammed the door shut, fearing that at any minute Tailspring's army would launch a physical attack on us. But closing the door did nothing to quell the noise. Surely the police would be arriving any second in response to the neighbor's complaints about someone being noisy next door. But no one showed up, and the noise continued for nearly ten minutes without pause. It finally ended as the Sun first glimmered on the horizon. After the howling ceased, we just looked at each other in total disbelief.

We uneasily made ourselves coffee and again asked Alexis just how she thought the cats had been the cause of her aunt's death. Sure, she had an unusual obsession and it was quite possible that she was suffering from some kind of psychological dependence on her new "family," but I still questioned why Alexis thought the cats had been the catalyst for Phyllis's demise. The strange event in the backyard remained unexplained, but we still couldn't make any solid link to Phyllis or her death. We got down to some hard-nosed research at this point and pored over the audiotapes for the next few hours. We narrowed the field down to three out of the twenty-seven tapes, that contained cat sounds, in which the recording sounded as though the cat noises were melding into human voices. One of the three contained continuous chatter that could have been background TV dialogue, and one was the original tape that Alexis had presented to Silvana. The latter was the most convincing. The third suspicious tape was a recording of a ceremony I recognized as a bastardized version of Egyptian cat worship spell casting that evoked the goddess Pasht, Bast's mirror sister. Black cats were considered especially sacred to Egyptians, so it made sense that Phyllis would be particularly enamored with them. As evidenced by the tapes and the notebooks, Phyllis was dabbling in occult disciplines that revered cats as conduits of superpowers and secrets. I agreed with Alexis that her aunt might have been attempting to gain some of these powers from the cats in her home, but even at that, Phyllis had still been using the cats as a positive force, not for destructive purposes.

Alexis maintained that the best she could offer was a gut feeling that all of this cat hocus-pocus had an evil intent and that it had ultimately caused her aunt's death. "Don't you see that she was manipulated by some outside force that centered around those cats. It was unnatural the way they would all come together when I entered the house, as if they were gathering and telling me not to intrude. It was also the way they looked at me—staring with unblinking green and yellow eyes that even glowed in the dark. I can't explain it, but they weren't normal house cats, and they were influencing my aunt's behavior. They made me feel very uncomfortable. You experienced that bizarre incident yourself last night didn't you? How do you explain that?" Alexis asked.

I couldn't explain it, and the best I could do at the moment was to say that we all needed a break—so I excused myself to go out front for some fresh air. I spotted Roger, one of the next door neighbors, puttering around on his lawn. I said hello and explained that we had stayed the night at Alexis's invitation. I then asked him if the cat racket had woken him last night.

"Racket? What racket?" he asked.

"Didn't you hear the cats howling at each other right before dawn? I thought they'd wake the whole neighborhood," I said.

"No, not at all. I got up around 3:30—I have trouble sleeping—but I didn't hear a thing. In fact, I let the dog out in the back and he surely would have heard cats howling," Roger told me. The neighbor went on to say that even when Phyllis was alive with her whole gang of cats in the house he had never seen them outside—except for the big one.

"You mean Tailspring?" I asked.

"Guess so . . . he was the leader. Funny thing though, Phyllis would never talk about him. She'd chatter about the other cats, but when I'd mention the big one I'd see in the yard now and again she'd just turn and walk away, almost as though he wasn't supposed to be mentioned," Roger told me.

I hurried back into the kitchen and told Silvana and Alexis that the neighbor hadn't heard the cats the night before. Alexis looked me straight in the eye and said, "You see, we all heard it because we are in this house, and those evil cats have some kind of power here." I looked to Silvana for support, but I realized she was at a loss for any explanation as well. We had all witnessed a wild event and Silvana and I had seen a huge black cat that Alexis confirmed from our description looked exactly like the missing Tailspring. But apparently we were the *only ones* who had experienced what happened. I was beginning to agree with Alexis that a paranormal event surrounding the cats was not impossible.

When I returned to the yard to see if the daylight uncovered any evidence of the cat battle we had heard in the night, there was absolutely no evidence of cat fur nor any smell of cat urine, once again providing no answer. This was even more disconcerting considering that the house had been full of cats not two weeks earlier. I tried another approach and asked Silvana if she was experiencing any new psychic disturbances, thinking that her abilities might provide some kind of a clue, but she said that there were no signs of anything. I concluded that whatever had caused last night's havoc had created it for one reason: to send us a message.

Vincent's office was able to obtain the coroner's report, which stated that Phyllis had died from ingesting an undetermined toxin that ultimately stopped her heart. The crime scene investigators described the death scene as showing no evidence of a break-in or struggle and from all apparent indications, Phyllis sat in her bed surrounded by the photos of her cats, took a poison, and died a relatively peaceful death. Forensics had found quite a bit of cat fur on the bed and on Phyllis, but that wasn't unusual considering she lived with nine cats. I reported these findings to Alexis as part of our investigation and told her that in most cases where a death occurs in an occult setting we can find some ceremonial paraphernalia like candles, incense, photos, even blood sacrifice. Phyllis's scene was squeaky clean. But I gave Alexis a bit of information that I discovered while researching cat mythology and folklore. One of the most common myths about cats is that they are capable of stealing the soul of a sleeping human if they are permitted to place their mouth near the person's face. It is said that the cat—especially the black cat—can literally take the breath from the person and inhale the human's soul, thus causing death. The legend harkens back to the hysterical fear of black cats as being demons in the service of the devil. Myths also tell of how during the witch hunts of the seventeenth and eighteenth centuries, pure black cats were summarily destroyed. Only cats anointed with white spots—"the finger of God"—were spared from horrible boilings, burnings, and dismemberment.

I didn't want to alarm Alexis; I just wanted to point out that over time there have been hundreds of myths and superstitions—both good and bad—linked to cats, and perhaps some of these tales were influencing her and possibly rationalizing her aunt's death in her own mind. Alexis could not come to grips with the fact that her aunt, who from all accounts loved life so much, would end it by her own hand.

Alexis maintained that before the cats came into her aunt's life she had never experienced the odd feelings of dread that permeated the house whenever she now entered it. She said she had always felt the atmosphere was comfortable and loving when Arnold had been alive. At first, when Phyllis adopted Tailspring, Alexis tolerated it despite the fact that Tailspring would often hiss at her, especially if it appeared as though Phyllis was taking time away from him. "Oh, don't mind him, dear," Phyllis would say to Alexis. "He just gets a little jealous." But as time went on and the number of cats mounted, they literally took over the house. "I dreaded going over there. Aunt Phyllis was not very kind when I got in the way of the cats. She would tell me that I should watch where I was walking, be careful not to disturb them when they were sleeping, or bother the area where she placed their food. I was on constant guard not to annoy her precious cats. And that big one, Tailspring, with those hideous yellow eyes, stared me down as though I was some kind of intruder," Alexis said.

Epilogue

We could not explain what had happened that night in Phyllis's backyard and unfortunately we never overcame Alexis's suspicion that the cats had "forced" Phyllis to take her own life by driving her mad or by using some supernatural power. In the days that followed, Alexis learned that her aunt's will was in fact enforced properly and although she was offered her aunt's house to live in, providing she would care for the cats, she declined and appointed a caretaker. She said that all of the cats were back in the house, including Tailspring. "Those green eyes still give me the creeps," she said.

I looked puzzled as we left Alexis, and as usual Silvana perceptively asked me what was wrong. "You have that look in your eye, Robert. I know you have something cooking in that head. Tell me what you are thinking now."

I said that it was quite a stretch, but my research showed that some cat magic was aimed at melding humans with their feline pets into one entity and that Phyllis might have been attempting to somehow metaphysically join herself with Tailspring.

"Oh, come on, Robert, that is even a bit much for you," Silvana responded.

I nodded my head in agreement, and then something dawned on me. I asked Silvana what color Alexis had said Tailspring's eyes were?

"She said they were green," Silvana answered.

"Yes, that's right. And that's what color the cat's eyes were the night we saw him in the yard, " I said.

"So, what is the big difference, Robert?"

"Don't you see? Alexis originally told us that Tailspring's yellow eyes frightened her when she visited her aunt. The cat we saw, and the Tailspring that was recently found, has *green* eyes," I said.

"Yes, that is right, the color has changed!" Silvana said.

"And what was Arnold's pet name for Phyllis?" I asked Silvana.

Silvana recalled that Arnold called Phyllis "Green Eyes"— Tailspring's new attribute.

10.

Houdini's Hellrats

Harry Houdini's gravesite always fascinated me. And when we got a chance to investigate a reported haunting of his West Coast retreat, I was thrilled at the possibility of becoming involved with anything related to the master. Little did I know that I'd walk away with some of the most convincing proof of the paranormal that X-Investigations had ever compiled.

As a boy, I was weaned on tales of how the legendary magician died during a death-defying illusion on Halloween—of all nights—in 1926. Over the years, I discovered that although he was the greatest magician of all time, many of Houdini's legendary feats of incredible prestidigitation were more the result of contortionist body movements than supernatural ability. But these revelations never tarnished the image of the great one in my mind; there were certainly hundreds, maybe thousands of other amazing illusions that Houdini did pull off, to the astonishment of people all over the world.

But the stuff of myths is powerful, and Houdini was, and is, a superhero of the mystical. Like all children, I idolized larger-than-life people, especially since I gravitated to the bizarre and supernatural even as a child. Aside from magicians like Houdini, I identified more with the dark powers of Dracula than the strength of Superman, and I would have rather controlled the elements of the universe like Dr. Strange, the master of the mystical arts, than have the supersenses of the amazing Spider-Man. But Houdini wasn't a fictional character. He was real, and despite knowing that what he did was nothing more than crafty illusion and misdirection, albeit masterfully, he was flesh and blood and a legend even among his magical peers, who often told of how Houdini mystified even them. Many of Houdini's acts could never be explained by other magicians of his day, and aside from his abilities on the stage, his magical *secrets* helped to create his supernatural mystique.

But what I believe has kept the legend of Harry Houdini alive and kept me so fascinated—even more so than have his wonderful accomplishments of magic and showmanship—is the compelling story of Houdini's séance. Whether it was the ultimate marketing ploy ever used in show business, or a sincere gesture to his wife, Bess (Wilhelmina) Rahner, the master magician, a recognized debunker of fraudulent mediums and psychics, made a pact with her that if there was any way possible to return from the dead, he would contact her.

And having lived so close to Houdini's gravesite in Queens, New York, I felt that my paranormal fate had determined I be close to the great one. Each Halloween until about a decade ago, after a traditional wand-breaking ceremony (signifying the end of a magician's career) at Houdini's gravesite in the Machpela Cemetery in Cypress Hills, Bess conducted a memorial séance in an effort to contact Houdini from beyond the grave. She thought that conducting a séance would be the best possible way for her departed husband to reconnect. One story tells that Houdini would ring a bell a number of times that only his wife would know to verify that it was really his spirit reaching out to her. As far as I can remember, Houdini never did make contact, but those in the world of the paranormal haven't given up. There are no shortages of theories about the afterlife, and one in particular states that we can never measure time as it applies to the spirit world because ghosts can be operating in a completely different time frame that we simply don't understand. So ... it leaves the Houdini contact possibility intact for believers and gives hope to paranormal investigators that some future séance may indeed pay off.

When fall settled in New York each year, I would brave the October 31 chill and make my way over to the Queens cemetery in an attempt to attend the ceremony and hopefully be invited to the Houdini séance afterward, now under the direction of Sidney H. Radner, a Houdini historian and collection curator. But that never came to pass (the séance was usually restricted to magicians of note and personal friends), so I was content to at least be in the "general vicinity" where something spectacular—in a paranormal sense—could possibly take place. I was happy to believe that Houdini would some day find a way to reach out, and I'd be there right alongside of him! I fantasized about his image appearing on a reality TV show and I would be an eyewitness to the event. This "delusion of grandeur" came back to me each time I'd conduct any investigation that focused on poltergeists or hauntings. I would think to myself that maybe the entity just might know where Houdini was hanging out in the afterlife and I could always ask if it had ever run into the late magician. This was my paranormal investigator's grand slam home run in the ninth inning. It was winning the Oscar at the Academy Awards. Being present for Houdini's great and mystical return that would stun the world—this was the stuff of dreams for me and many of my colleagues.

Radner holds the séance each year at a location that had some significance to Houdini's life. The event has become a grand sit-down dinner affair with speeches and testimonials followed by the séance. I often thought that Houdini would probably have wanted to avoid all of the hoopla of second-rate magicians and that if he did return from the dead, he would do it in a much more spectacular way—maybe in Times Square on New Year's Eve. But I was just jealous, and after years of pleasant but frustrating Houdini spirit watching in New York, I got used to the idea that it would be a long shot for sure to ever experience the ultimate ghost encounter. And after leaving the gravesite on a particularly cold and gloomy Halloween evening in 1996, the neighborhood surroundings put me in mind of my old high school pal, Tony, with whom I raised quite a bit of hell as teenagers in Queens.

Tony had moved to Los Angeles some years ago and became a successful glamour photographer, shooting some of the most beautiful models in the world. But unlike me, Tony was very down to earth. As a photographer focusing on physical beauty, his interest in the flesh outweighed any leanings he might have toward the mysteries of the spirit. But Tony always humored me and would politely feign interest in my paranormal ramblings. When I told him about X-Investigations, he shook his head, raised his hands, and wiggled his fingers in a comical "booga, booga" gesture. But despite his skeptical attitude when it came to the unknown, Tony was a good friend and he volunteered to join me as the case photographer if I had any "ghost busting" to do in the Los Angeles area. "Sure, I'll take pictures of ghosts and goblins for you as long as you can guarantee to get Casper's agent to let me get a shot of him lounging at the pool," Tony quipped in vintage Brooklynese.

I made it a point to give him a call the next day to touch base and to reminisce about the old neighborhood again. It had been months since we last spoke and with the chill of the fall in the air, the memories of the new school year resurrected some fond old memories of how Tony and I would plan to meet girls, skip school, and scheme how to get enough money to "hang out."

"Hey, Anthony," I yelled into the phone when he answered my call the next day. "What's goin' on over there in Hollywood? Still taking pictures of half-naked women?"

Tony was glad to hear from me. Every time we talk, we inevitably compare notes about which of us has a more bizarre lifestyle. It's a game we've always played—he tells me about the psycho model who ran naked from his studio near the on ramp of Interstate 405, and I tell him about how Silvana psychically discovered that her latest beau was related to an ex-Nazi war criminal. I admit that I embellished some of these stories, and I'm certain Tony did too.

"So what's going on in your world?" he asked me. I mentioned some of our more recent cases—werewolves in Van Nuys, vampires in Transylvania, and ghosts in Salem—the regular stuff that Tony expected to hear and because of our long relationship, he never even raised an eyebrow at their outrageousness. And I expected to hear some wild Hollywood party story from Tony about sex, drugs, and what ingénue did what to the hottest new stud boy. But Tony surprised me this time. He began by recounting some photography yarn but then stopped in midstream. "Hey, I almost forgot. I have a story that's right up your alley. You're going to love this one. I couldn't believe it when I heard it, but I knew this was one that you'd go crazy over," he said.

My curiosity was piqued because Tony was a jaded sort when it came to shocking revelations, especially since we went back so far, so his enthusiasm got me jazzed. "So tell me already. What is it?"

"Well, I was shooting this young woman for a catalog session in my studio recently and when we broke for lunch sitting around the reception area she saw your book *Corporate Magick* sitting on the coffee table. I guess she's into all of your witchy mumbo jumbo because she picked it up, started reading it, and saying things like it was cool and all. So I told her that I knew you and how you guys are investigating ghosts and the paranormal and then she really got excited. She told me that she has been very sensitive to paranormal events all of her life, having seen the ghosts of her grandparents and being able to pick up on hauntings in people's houses and things like that. She mentioned to me that her friends call her 'Polty'—short for poltergeist, because she's always telling them about her weird experiences," Tony said.

Anyone who's nicknamed after a poltergeist is someone I want to hear about, so I got comfortable and asked Tony to give me all of the details about Polty. He said that it wasn't so much Polty that I'd be interested in but the Hollywood celebrity ghost story that the woman had to tell. "I tell you, Bobby, this one even gave me the creeps—and I immediately thought this would be a great case for you to look into," Tony said.

"So what's so creepy about it? There are hundreds of Hollywood hauntings that I'm aware of and I'm sure there are even more that no one has ever heard of. What makes this one so special?" I asked.

Tony didn't say anything for about fifteen seconds—just to further whet my appetite. "It's about your favorite magician of all time . . . Harry Houdini . . . and the woman claims that she had made contact with spirits that hang around his old abandoned house out here in Hollywood. She said that she's gone to the ruins of the house many times and each time she goes she picks up on some new kind of ghost or demon or something. You know, I talk to a lot of crazies out here, from New Age nuts to people claiming they're aliens, but this girl seems real sincere—and her stories are spine tingling."

I wanted to know more about Polty's Houdini paranormal experiences, and Tony recounted what he could remember. Polty had decided to visit the Walker Mansion, the ruins of a house owned by Dr. Ralph Walker, a friend of Houdini and his wife, where they had often visited. It is unknown how long Houdini actually stayed at the mansion, but records indicate that Bess and her manager, Edward Saint, took up residence in the guest house on the estate. The mansion ruins is at the foot of Laurel Canyon Boulevard and Lookout Mountain Drive. The house burned down in 1959, but the guesthouse where the Houdinis stayed remained standing. The property is the first site visible on the right side of the road when one heads into Hollywood over the "hill" from the San Fernando Valley. Most people would never know that the master illusionist ever spent time at the place, which now looks like it was hit by a bomb. A short time ago, however, much of the property was bought and restored by Hollywood stars Billy Bob Thornton and Angelina Jolie, but it managed to retain its mysterious reputation as Houdini's house.

Tony went on recounting Polty's story. She had become fascinated with Houdini's reputation for exposing fake mediums and paranormal charlatans, and because she believed herself to be genuine she admired the magician's techniques. Tony noted that it was her method of psychologically assuring herself that she had bona fide powers. If she could pass Houdini's historical psychic scam tests, then she would be able to profess her genuine abilities. So when Polty decided to visit the Walkers ruins, she prepared herself to be the conduit of any and all spiritual entities or vibrations, especially if they were connected to Houdini in any way. She read voraciously about Houdini's life and career and each time she met with Tony at a photo shoot she told him some new tidbit of information or minutiae concerning Houdini's life, especially if it was at all connected to the Walker property. Polty discovered that a key had been found buried under the ruins during an excavation of the land that was said to be the key to Bess's guesthouse. "If I could only get my hands on that key, I know I could contact Houdini," she often told Tony. He said that she had become totally obsessed with Houdini and she claimed that she wouldn't rest until she made "contact" with his spirit.

I was glad to hear about Polty's paranormal leanings, but I pressed Tony on telling me why he thought I'd be so interested on a professional and personal level. I expected to hear that Polty channeled Houdini's spirit during a séance or that she had somehow made contact with him. I also expected to hear that she was the only witness to these events and Tony bought the stories because of Polty's convincing manner. Tony loved a good story, and I knew as a lifelong buddy that a pretty young woman would always get his ear. But what

Tony told me was more intriguing than I expected. He told me that Polty indeed made contact with the other side after her visit to the Walker ruins in Hollywood, but it wasn't with Houdini, or with Bess for that matter. Polty was being haunted by entities she described as "hellrats."

The Hellrats

"What on earth is a hellrat?" I asked Tony after he told me that strange ratlike ghost creatures had been victimizing Polty for weeks since she had visited the Walker ruins. Polty told Tony that she had visited the historical property a number of times during her quest to make contact with Houdini's spirit, to no avail. She would visit the site late at night so as not to arouse suspicion from the local police or neighbors and walk among the ruins until she "felt" a special psychic vibe where she thought the magician's spirit might be. Polty had visited the place for ten nights straight, even pitching a tent on the grounds one Friday evening so she could spend the entire night. "She told me that she got these little vibrations of some kind of spirits or ghosts, or something that made her keep coming back. She thought it was Houdini sending her little messages and that eventually he would appear to her and make contact with her," Tony said.

But after spending many long hours on the dark creepy grounds overgrown with foliage, dotted with damaged cement grottos, and paths that led to nowhere, Polty was about to give up hope, until the night she fell asleep under the stone arch that mysteriously compelled her to return, night after night. The arch, which can barely be seen from the road, was the entranceway to a path that led up a hill to what was once a large outdoor gathering place. The dirt pathway had long since been covered by natural debris and bursting tree roots, but Polty sensed that it was the central point for large gatherings of people in times past. She had strong psychic vibrations of human souls. But what Polty couldn't immediately figure out was the distinctly "inhuman" auras that permeated the area, too. Tony told me that Polty said that she felt that there were many people who had participated in the parties or rituals in the area and that they had all passed through the archway, but she couldn't explain the other vibrations. "She said they felt similar to the vibes she got from the zoo," Tony said.

Polty awoke at sunrise and was surprised that she had fallen asleep under the archway because she didn't remember being that tired or dozing off. She went home, showered, and went about her business for the day. Her visit to the Houdini ruins stayed with her throughout the day the way a particularly vivid dream haunts your workaday subconscious. She had a mixed feeling of psychic satisfaction and a sense of dread whenever the memory entered her mind. She brushed it off for most of the day and concentrated on her modeling, but her problems began to worsen that night.

The model prepared herself for bed in her usual manner, bathing, moisturizing, and brushing her hair. She left her bathroom and picked up the rock on her hall table that she had taken from the Walker ruins as a memento. The memories of the night before slammed into her head in a rush of color and sensory overload so intense that she became dizzy and nearly lost her balance. She recalled the psychic vibrations and once again felt the human souls, but this time she could identify the "other" vibes. They were distinct this time ... Polty sensed the presence of animals, not pets, but wild creatures that she saw in her mind's eye growling, snarling, and tearing at human flesh in a crazed rabid frenzy.

Tony told me that Polty described the event in graphic detail. She said she could see hundreds of giant ratlike animals with yellow eyes running through the Houdini grotto squeaking an unearthly shrill. They overran the grounds like a sea of grey and black fur, their heads picking and gnawing at anything or anyone that got in their path. The hellrats climbed trees and overran the stone walls and archways of the grottos, leaving a gooey brown-red trail that Polty said looked like blood. But the flashback was only the beginning of Polty's problem. She sat down in her living room chair to regain her composure. Once the dizziness stopped, Polty assured herself that what had just occurred was nothing more than some kind of dream intruding on reality, probably caused by the stress of her day and her lack of sleep over the weeks she spent much of the night at the Walker Mansion site. She went to bed, only to be awakened around 3:00 A.M. by a clicking noise. It first sounded as though someone was tapping on the bedroom door. But as she gained consciousness, she could hear that the tapping was coming from inside the wall behind her bed's headboard. She sat up and listened as the tapping increased. Just when she was about to swing her legs around and jump out of her bed, the tapping stopped ... and the squeaking began. The sickening shrill of the hellrats in her dreamlike episode just hours ago could now be heard from the walls of her bedroom. She was paralyzed by the sounds and thought that any moment the disgusting creatures would burst through and devour her flesh.

I told Tony that this story was incredible and asked him if he believed what Polty had told him. He said that from everything he knew about her, aside from her claims of being psychic, she was a normal person. And when she was telling him the story, she had been visibly upset. "She's lost weight, gotten very pale, and started chain smoking," he told me.

"Over what could have been a nightmare?" I asked him.

"No way. That's only part of it. That's only the beginning, Bobby. Polty got spooked big time, and it wasn't by a dream, my friend."

I learned that a few days later Polty came late to one of Tony's photo shoots looking more disturbed than ever. She was not only physically drained and gaunt, but she was now acting what Tony described as "wired and paranoid." When he asked her why she was freaking out, Polty told Tony that the event in her apartment was just the first of a series of strange things that she was experiencing. The creatures she had envisioned were haunting her every night at all hours, constantly waking her from sleep. "They scratch at the walls and I can see them scurry through my apartment on the floor, then up the walls. But they don't go into holes—they're huge and could never fit. They go right through the ceiling and through the medicine cabinet mirror like they're invisible, Tony. I'm not losing my mind. They're really haunting me," she had told him.

The story was still hard to take, and although I always enjoyed visiting with Tony, we had been talking for the better part of an hour; my "unlimited" minutes were beginning to add up. I started to politely end the conversation when Tony said, "Hold on, buddy. I know this story sounds wild, but listen to what happened next."

"So what happened? Polty sounds like she has some problems, but where's the paranormal part come in?"

"She had rat bites on her arms—huge ones. I saw them. And her doctor, who's my doctor, too, confirmed it. She had to get rabies shots and everything. She said the rats from her dreams bit her. And the crazy part is that she insists the rats are ghost rats from hell," Tony said. He went on to add that Polty had told him that during one of her more intense psychic episodes at the Walker ruins, she began getting flashes of the magician conducting a ceremony that she had first thought was nothing more than one of his magical performances. But as she saw more, she realized that it wasn't Houdini at all, but another man, dressed in a red robe with a white hood, who appeared to be holding a gray animal by its hind legs over a pit in a stone grotto.

Polty claimed that the more times she visited the ruins, the more intense her vibes became, to the point where she could not resist going there every night. She was frightened that somehow she had opened the doorway to the afterlife through a gateway that exists on the Walker site that may have been some kind of sacred—perhaps evil—magical sanctuary. She thought that her relentless attempts to contact Houdini might have inadvertently opened a pathway to reach other spirits that inhabited the grounds. She was convinced that she had stumbled on a vortex between this world and the next and the rats—the "hellrats"—were guardians of the vortex and protected it from intruders.

"So Polty thinks the rats identified her as an intruder and are warning her to stay away?" I asked.

"Yup, that's what she thinks. She's terrified that they will haunt her until she dies or goes mad. She can describe them to a tee. She said they are as big as a raccoon, but with larger heads and sharp, pointy faces—a cross between a possum and a giant rat."

"But what's her proof?" I asked, this time insisting on a clincher to the tale.

"As a matter of fact, she has pictures," he said.

Okay, so now I was hooked. And I told Tony to have Polty contact me if she was interested in having the help of X-Investigations. Perhaps we could flush out any possible paranormal event or haunting that may have been affecting her life since her contact at the Walker grounds. I reminded Tony that my associate Silvana is a "sensitive" who possesses ultrapsychic abilities and can often feel things the way Polty claimed she did. But Tony said Polty was much too disturbed to bring anyone else into her situation and that the only reason she had told him about it was that they had a mutual acquaintance in their physician and because she had confided in Tony about her Houdini house fascination even before the bizarre events began. Coupled with the fact that Polty did not have much money to spend on "paranormal assistance," Tony was confident that the model wouldn't ask for our help. But he suggested that if I was really interested I could always take a trip out to Los Angeles and stay with him. And, of course, while I was there I could take a ride over to the Walker grounds myself and check it out. "I know you're fascinated with Houdini. Now's your chance to see where he hung out and maybe bust some ghosts while you're at it," Tony said convincingly. He added, "Yeah, and you can bring Silvana along with you, too, there's plenty of room here."

"Oh, so that's it. You want to see Silvana again don't you?" I said. Tony had a thing for my psychic sidekick ever since he had met her on one of his trips back to New York to visit relatives. But I couldn't blame him for requesting her presence. Silvana is a beauty—tall, curvy, with long, black hair and striking dark features—and Tony was always looking for women like Silvana to photograph. When she wears her signature leather "catwoman" jumpsuit, she looks like a cross between a comic book superheroine and Elvira. "Don't tell me you made up this whole story just to get Silvana to take her clothes off?" I asked snidely.

"Nah, this is the real deal for your kind of business. You'll find some spooks at that place for sure. And tell Silvana to bring her bikini," Tony responded.

Houdini's Haunted Grounds

Tony lived in a proper feng shui Japanese-style house in Sherman Oaks, a well-to-do section of the San Fernando Valley. Silvana and I arrived on a Saturday afternoon and, after a good New York Italian meal, Tony suggested that we head over to the Walker grounds and take a look. Polty declined Tony's invitation to meet us, partly out of embarrassment and partly due to what Tony described as her apprehension about bringing any more of the wrath of the hellrats down on her. Polty's mental state was very fragile and the last thing we wanted to do was force an investigation on someone who's disturbed. And in any investigation that involves hauntings or possessions, we will first scout out the affected areas to be sure we know how to proceed with the case. Although new technology has decreased much of the bulk of the typical "ghost buster" paraphernalia, there are still a number of pieces of electronic equipment and connections that must be applied to capture "proof" of an entity or event. We also knew that this was an outdoor situation, so it would require special infrared lighting and scopes, along with supersensitive listening devices. More important, X-Investigations' most valuable and indispensable scouting device is not a piece of equipment at all, but Silvana's very human psychic gift. So with nothing more than directions from Polty to the Walker ruins and Silvana's fine-tuned mind, we made the trip over the "hill" just as dusk was settling over the City of Angels.

I was shocked. I had expected to see a house on top of the embankment that was described in historical Los Angeles literature, but what was standing on the corner of Coldwater Canyon was a shell. From the street all that could be clearly seen were the surrounding stone walls and the paths that led up a steep hill toward the back of the house. On our trip over, Tony had told us some of the legends of the Houdini house (however, he hadn't known that Houdini never actually lived there) about secret passageways that ran under the property across the road and into what was then film star Fatty Arbuckle's home. Tony said the two celebrities used to run concurrent parties, shuttling guests (usually ingénues) between their soirees.

We parked the car as inconspicuously as we could. I thought to myself that Polty must have been doing plenty of sneaking around to be able to visit the grounds so often and to stay there overnight on a number of occasions. Most of the accessible property could easily be seen from the roadside, so entry and exit were not hidden. But it fit with L.A.'s reputation of people ignoring pedestrians. No one walks in L.A., and those who do are virtually invisible.

We took along a few flashlights and, after being stopped in our tracks by some barking dogs from a neighboring property, we continued on and climbed a small wall about three feet high at one side of the lot. Despite the car headlights from the nearby road, most of the hill in front of us was dark and we needed the flashlights just to see our footsteps in front of us. Silvana noted that the brush smelled deeply of lilac and roses (her sense of smell was as good as her sixth sense) and the further we walked up the hill the more we could smell the fresh, wet earth. I pointed out to our scouting party that there was a distinct animal odor on the hill, reminiscent of wet dog. Tony told us that there are a number of different kinds of animals, especially coyotes and possums, that come down from the mountains and run through the area foraging for food.

When we got closer to the top of the hill, I could see the outline of the stone arch Polty had described to Tony. I said to Silvana that it looked like we were headed in the right direction, and I asked her to try to pick up any disturbances. Wasting no time, she sat down on a nearby rock, lowered her head, and began to meditate. Tony and I no doubt looked quite silly standing in the darkness holding flashlights on each other as Silvana went deep into her mind, but I whispered to him that this was the way we'd find out if the grounds were really haunted. My boyhood pal was becoming obviously apprehensive at the prospect of seeing or hearing real ghosts. He shuffled back and forth, saying that maybe we should leave before the police found us trespassing.

"I didn't see any signs, Tony. Are you just a little nervous now that we're entering the afterlife? A little scared of ghosts are you, big guy?" I said sarcastically, looking to get a rise out of my friend.

By this time, Silvana had cleared her mind and was completely tuned in to the surrounding area. Before I asked her any questions, I shone the flashlight toward her. After working closely with Silvana for so many years, I could always tell by her facial expression whether there was any reason for concern. She would squint and lower her head a few inches. When things were *really* worrisome, she joined her hands in sort of a fisted prayer clench. As I raised the beam of light from her knees upward, I saw the telltale fist, the lowered tilt of her head, and her squint. "It's bad, Silvana?" I asked.

"Robert, there is something here to be afraid of. The energy is old and it has sinned greatly. We are not wanted here. I do not believe the presence wants any living thing to set foot on these grounds again. There has been much death and suffering. So much so that the earth has been scorched so it could be cleansed," Silvana said.

The word *scorched* made me remember that the 1959 fire that destroyed the building might have been deliberately set in an effort to purify some decadent and blasphemous history surrounding the Walker Mansion and Houdini's old haunt. But before I could explain my hypothesis, Silvana suggested that we leave that very moment. Before I could respond to her plea, Tony was trotting down the hill ten feet ahead of us. Silvana followed him, but I stayed a few moments longer and directed the flashlight beam toward the top of the hill and the stone archway. I was sure this was the archway Polty had described to Tony, so I wanted to have some navigational bearing in my mind for our next visit to the ruins. The case now had some real meat to it in my mind and I was convinced there was further merit to continue the paranormal investigation.

We arrived back at Tony's home close to 11:30 that night. It seemed uncommonly cold and damp for L.A., but Tony assured me that the hills get a lot cooler than most people think.

"Maybe we have brought some dead spirits with us to make the air cold," Silvana quipped.

"Please, I've had enough cold bodies in this house—and I don't mean dead ones either," Tony shot back at her.

We all decided that the Walker property reeked of some odd presence. Silvana absolutely sensed something amiss, my gut feelings said there was a case to be pursued, and even Tony, who was a complete civilian in the paranormal world, agreed that there was a spooky feel about the grounds that made him feel very uncomfortable and unwanted. We also agreed that there was a strong possibility that Polty was experiencing some odd manifestations as a result of her obsession with the area.

Silvana pointed out that gifted people like herself, and possibly Polty, have an advantage over others in accessing another dimension or the spirit world by virtue of their inherent power. "It is like having a key to the lock before you even know what door to open," she explained.

And when these extrasensory types are intent on something, or someone specific, all hell can break loose. They can literally open the door so wide that they let in the whole ghostly neighborhood!

Before we contacted Polty, I decided that Silvana and I would do another preliminary investigation of the site to confirm our suspicions. If we had positive results, we could then ask Polty to join us in a concerted attempt to "bust" whatever was troubling Polty's life. If she had inadvertently released some malevolent beings, she should not be held responsible. If she had purposely released them, then we'd have to convince her to try to send them back. But our first mission was to get some hard evidence to present to her.

Armed with a series of recorders, cameras, and electronic metering devices, Silvana and I loaded Tony's SUV the next evening and bid him a good night as we pulled out of his driveway on our way to the Walker ruins. We parked in the same secluded area and trudged up the same path as the night before. Silvana said that she was sensing the same dreadful vibes and because she had already made psychic connections, she was experiencing them without the need to meditate. "They are powerful, Robert," she said as we got closer to the grotto archway at the top of the hill. "Be very careful. I am feeling the badness . . . the sad blackness," she warned, as I shone the flashlight upward.

As much as I admired Silvana's psychic power and appreciated her immeasurable value to our team, I was often glad that I couldn't feel the many conflicting emotions and malevolent thoughts she could tune in to because of her ESP. She would often leave an event completely drained and so upset that she would tell me I didn't want to know what she had just experienced. From her apparent apprehension as we approached the archway, I knew this was one of those times that Silvana wished she was simply "normal."

She helped me set up some of our cameras and lights and pleaded, "Please hurry. The police may come."

I said, "What, are you getting like Tony? What are you afraid of?"

Silvana shook her head—a signal that we should get the hell out of there, fast!

Within fifteen minutes we snapped some photos, checked our meters, and recorded all of the ambient sounds. Nothing seemed out of the ordinary except a sudden spike in our Gauss meter that registered a significant change in the electromagnetic field in the area. I discounted it as a reaction to a camera flash that went off at the same moment. So, heeding Silvana's plea, we quickly packed up and left the Walker property the same way we entered it . . . curious, but with no real evidence.

That's what I first thought. The next morning we had the luxury of using Tony's darkroom in his photography studio to develop the film we had shot. Most of the photos of the surrounding area showed unkempt brush, dirt roads, and stone ruins. We had taken at least thirty photos of the hilltop archway—some of it alone and some with me standing underneath to give a point of reference. As we looked over the shots, we were happy to see that the quality was excellent, but dismayed as to the lack of anything we would consider evidence of the paranormal. Tony came in and looked over our shoulders at the drying prints. He asked if we'd got anything last night, and I said, "Not really. Just some good shots of Houdini's old West Coast haunt."

Just then, Tony took out his loop—a professional magnifying piece for photo slides. He pressed the loop down onto one of the prints and said, "Holy shit!"

"What? What do you see?" I asked.

"You mean you didn't see this?"

"See what?" I asked again and then took the loop from his hand, bending down to take a closer look at what he was talking about. I pressed the loop down onto the still damp photo and what I saw caused my eyes to widen in disbelief.

In one of the photos taken of me standing under the stone archway, an animal's head seemingly embedded into the stone can clearly be seen peering down at me. The creature looked exactly as Polty had described it—the head was gray and black and had a long pointed face, like a rat's. The beady coal-black eyes stared down at me from the top of the arch as though it was warning me to stay away. Neither I, nor Silvana, had seen anything in real time as we took the photograph, but there in the actual print we had proof of the existence of Polty's hellrats!

Epilogue

Polty didn't need to see the proof. We weren't able to meet with her in L.A., so we phoned her when we arrived back in New York. She said that she wasn't surprised about what we had seen in the photo and that we should be thankful that the picture was the only manifestation of the hellrat that intruded on our lives. She told me mournfully, "I pushed it. I tried to communicate with entities that live in that area who simply don't want to be disturbed. I don't know if Houdini's ghost had anything to do with it or not, but the place is definitely haunted by dozens, maybe hundreds of spirits—some that are not so pleasant. Don't you think it's odd that they never conduct the annual Halloween séance there? I won't go back, and I suggest you stay away, too. After all, we have been warned."

II.

Andrea's Strangler

What do you say to well-to-do parents who claim their eight-year-old daughter, a privileged child in a private school with every creature comfort imaginable, is being haunted by the ghost of a deranged strangler?

Queries regarding hauntings top the list of calls received by X-Investigations. After only three months of operation, our office got a haunted house or ghost sighting call at least once a day. A majority of the calls were from people who were possibly very bored, a little loony, or simply paranormal "jerky boy" telephone pranksters. Silvana and I called the bulk of these "potential clients" the "spook kooks," because invariably their stories were almost identical. They would begin with either a haunted house they had spent the night in or an apparition floating around their house causing all kinds of disturbing and disruptive havoc. Very few of these stories hit a chord. It's usually not what has been experienced but more the sound of the caller's voice—a frightened, harrowing tone.

This is how Steven and Karen sounded when Silvana got their call one sunny July morning in 1999.

Because of her psychic sight, Silvana is more finely aware of the honesty in people's tales. She has a built-in "bullshit meter" that's specifically tuned into the paranormal worlds, so in addition to immediately being able to dismiss the crazies, Silvana can go to another level and discern whether a person's claim has some legitimacy. I often thought it was just a matter of her being involved in the occult for so many years that she had naturally developed wisdom, but on almost all occasions Silvana's instincts were uncanny. So when she entered my office that morning with a blanched look and told me about the Virginia couple's problem, I knew we had a hard-core haunting on our hands.

Steven and Karen told us at a meeting in their home later that week that they had been extremely happy and fortunate to have been able to buy the "house of their dreams" in such a good neighborhood in this Virginia suburb not far from metropolitan Washington, D.C. Both federal government workers, the couple and their eight-year-old daughter, Andrea, were settling into the big gray Victorian house they called the "Gray Lady" to start their lives on a secure foundation. Steven explained that the family had relocated from Minneapolis and had looked for months to find just the right house in the right neighborhood with good schools for Andrea. Steven and Karen took turns flying to Virginia on weekends to do their house hunting months before their transfers came through. But they hadn't been able to find a house they liked and more important could afford. "We love

Victorians, and in the better neighborhoods the prices were prohibitive," Steven said.

The House

But their luck changed when their broker called and told them that a large Victorian—just their style—had just become available after the previous family had to move suddenly. "It's gonna go fast," the broker told Steven. He advised them to catch the next plane and check it out. The young couple took his advice and made the trip the very next day, checkbook in hand. The house was everything they wanted, and they immediately fell in love. "I said to Steven that the price *had* to be ridiculous and the broker just lured us here to rope us in. But to our shock and joy, the house was affordable. We were thrilled," Karen said.

But they both knew there had to be a catch somewhere. A beautiful house in a great neighborhood priced a $100,000 under market value? Something had to be wrong. And indeed, something was wrong. The broker laughed and explained that the "Gray Lady" had a "silly history" of causing strange behavior in its inhabitants. After pressing the broker, Steven learned that within eighteen months' time, three families had left the house in the lurch. The broker didn't get into the details, but during their lunch at a local diner the couple discovered from the diner owner that the father of a prior resident had been committed to a mental hospital after living in the house for only a few months, having suffered a breakdown that was said to be "business related." And the previous family's young son had been arrested and incarcerated for mutilating local animals, forcing that family to leave the neighborhood.

"Very bizarre," Karen said to the diner owner.

"Yes," he responded, "but it's the choking that gets everyone the most."

"The choking?" Steven asked.

The owner said, "That's right, sir. No one can be in that house for more than a few days without feeling like they're bein' strangled. No workers, utility people . . . and especially no one who lives there. Everyone feels like their throat's closin' up on 'em at some point. Some think it has to do with some kinda mold in the house that's makin' everyone sick, but there's too many strange coincidences that go on there, too. Crazy house, that Gray Lady."

We all sat in silence for a moment transfixed by this part of Steven's story. By now, Steven had buried his head in his hands and was holding back tears. Silvana looked my way with a glance that I recognized as her signal that Steven was the real deal and his story was about to get even more bizarre. I asked him to continue, and he told me what was truly troubling him. They had decided to move into the house despite the stories and rumors because they felt it was a deal they couldn't pass up. They rationalized all the "spook stories" and the choking tales as a small community's urban legend and, like most intelligent types, they thought that they'd find the solution to the house's history and after time dispel all the crazy notions of hauntings and a weird presence.

"A 'weird presence'?" I asked Steven.

"Well, yes. That was the beginning. We were fine moving into the house. Our daughter, Andrea, loved her new room and we settled in rather quickly. But one evening at about ten o'clock, after Andrea had gone to bed, we were watching TV when it began. Karen was dozing off and I wasn't far behind her. The room was dark except for the light from the TV and I lowered the sound so as to not disturb Karen. But I then had the feeling that someone was in the room. You know, that sense that someone's watching you? I almost didn't want to turn around but something made me look. I sat up and turned my head slowly. At first I thought I had been half asleep, but then my eyes focused on Andrea, at the top of the stairs and looking as though she was sleep walking. She stood there, not moving, and I asked her what she was doing out of bed and if she was all right. She looked at me with a dazed expression, raised her hand to her throat, and said, 'Daddy, my throat feels like it's closing. I need some water.' Before I could get to the top of the stairs, Andrea fell to her knees, choking and gasping for air. I held her and tried to do CPR but she began to turn blue. I called for Karen in a panic and could do nothing but shake Andrea in my arms as I tried to get her to respond. I was totally panicked," Steven said.

The little girl finally responded and recovered her breath. The relieved parents asked her if she was all right and were astounded by Andrea's response. "She said to us that the man in her room brought her to the top of the stairs and said if we didn't destroy the house and the grounds, he would strangle her. Of course, we thought this was Andrea hallucinating from lack of oxygen or maybe she had had a bad dream. We didn't press it right away because we didn't want to frighten her any more than she already was," Karen recounted.

Andrea was checked by a physician and appeared fine. After a few days, her parents asked her about the "man in her room." The young girl stuck to her story and claimed that she had heard a thump in her bedroom closet and then an elderly man, with a scruffy beard, disheveled white hair, and dressed in denim farmer's overalls had walked into her room. He was carrying a thick yellow rope, dirty and stained with a dark red, almost black substance that could have been dried oil or maybe blood, according to the child's description. Karen said that Andrea asked him who he was and what he wanted, but the man just took her by the hand and led her to the top of the stairs. That's when Steven saw her and the choking began. "We did all we could—doctors and psychologists—and we talk to Andrea constantly and assure her everything's okay. But now that things have gotten worse, we're at our wit's end. That's why we think there's a strange entity of some kind affecting our lives. I know it sounds like something out of a *Poltergeist* movie, but Andrea has never lied to us. She's had these choking things three more times and we hear noises from the attic in the middle of the night. There's a bang, then walking sounds, and also some kind of creaking like a loose floorboard or a bending branch," Karen said.

Silvana and I digested the couple's story that afternoon and told them we'd return the next day. We considered that maybe they were under some kind of suggestion hysteria caused by the town ghost stories. Silvana continued to believe that they were sincere based on all of the psychic vibes she was getting. And we both agreed that they did not appear the type of people who would put their only daughter in jeopardy or make her the butt of a fabrication for the sake of some kind of notoriety. After all, they were financially comfortable and from all appearances were quite normal. The parents didn't want to put Andrea through any more trauma than she had already experienced, so we agreed not to interview the girl but to take her parents' testimony at face value. The family had kept detailed notes comprising nearly sixty-five pages of Andrea's conversations with the old man. Each time she spoke with him, she said the apparition would begin to speak to her but could never finish a sentence. He would literally be stuck on words and could not explain himself, according to Andrea's reports.

We had done some more fieldwork and had discovered school records (compliments of Vincent's agency's crack detectives) that the eight year old was a very intelligent and perceptive child. Some reports indicated that she often knew the answer to a question before her teacher would even ask it. Andrea was also prone to "creating" other worlds and "fantasy people," whom she claimed she conversed with and told her about things that were going to happen and things from the past that an eight year old couldn't possibly have known—to the astonishment of her teachers. Her precognitive abilities were categorized as simply being "acute sensitivity and an especially keen awareness of her environment"—fancy terms for extrasensory perception. Silvana read between the lines and said that Andrea was "apparently very gifted with PSI abilities—very much like when I was a little girl, Robert."

So the question was no longer whether Andrea was experiencing a paranormal event, but from where it was originating. The facts pointed to local legends purporting "choking incidents" among former residents of the house, spontaneous choking with visible welts on Andrea's neck, sudden and continuous noises from the attic area over the girl's bedroom, and Andrea's own testimony regarding discussions with an old man with a rope just prior to her choking episodes. We reported back to Steven and Karen that our investigation should continue, with Silvana and I staying at the house and using our equipment in an effort to capture what was troubling the family. We decided that we'd be introduced to Andrea as friends of the family who were going to spend the night. Fortunately, the guest bedroom was directly across from Andrea's room, which allowed us to set up cameras and sound-recording instruments near the "action."

Facing the Strangler

It was nearly dawn before Silvana awoke. We had spent the night in the room across from Andrea's and had not experienced anything unusual. I had stayed awake to monitor the equipment and occasionally peek in on Andrea as she slept. It was still dark outside when I saw the time was 4:58 A.M. on my digital watch. I was disappointed that we had come up with nothing, but then I reminded myself that in most of our investigations we spend days, sometimes weeks, before we solve the problem or close the case. I realized I was too anxious and was at least glad that Silvana had slept comfortably. I thought that maybe I should grab a few winks myself when suddenly Silvana awoke with a start and sat straight up in the bed. "It is here!" she shouted. I stood up, startled, and asked her what she was talking about. She shushed me and said to listen. Dead silence. Silvana looked toward the ceiling as she pointed to the door. "It is entering her room now, Robert," Silvana whispered. "Listen, it is rumbling. The en-te-te is a-va-ka-ning," Silvana said, emphasizing each hard letter in her full-on Czech accent.

I listened hard and heard what sounded like a low banging coming from the attic. The sound changed to a shuffling and grew progressively louder. I checked the equipment to make sure everything was recording. We had microphones in the room along with a video monitor. We had also set up a remote control still camera outside of the house focused on the top of the house and the window of Andrea's room.

Silvana rushed to the guest room door and pushed it open. "The thing is in there," she shouted. We ran across the hall and flung Andrea's door open to find the child in her bed, turned toward the window and speaking. "What, what do you want me for?" she said in a teary voice. By this time, Steven and Karen had hurried to the room as well. I stopped them from rushing on to Andrea's side, asking that they wait just a moment and listen to their child's voice. I had to restrain Steven's natural fatherly instinct to help his daughter, explaining that we were finally getting to the bottom of this problem.

Silvana had become completely immersed in a trance, desperately trying to intercede with whatever was holding Andrea's attention. But the child kept crying and asking what the old man wanted. She was rocking back and forth on her bed staring at the space between her and the bedroom window, its apparent emptiness belied by the girl's intent focus. Daylight was beginning to break outside the window and despite the noise we were making in her doorway, Andrea was oblivious to our presence. We managed to quiet down, and I glanced over at the equipment monitors to make sure everything was functioning properly. I was glad that I had remembered to activate the outdoor motion shutter release on the still Nikon camera before I had left the guest room. The camera was now snapping pictures of the house every three seconds.

We could all hear Andrea speaking to whatever was in her room but we couldn't make out any response. It was difficult keeping Karen quiet and back from her daughter's side. The woman kept praying to herself and asking how this could be happening to her little girl. Steven finally convinced her to quiet down, and then we heard the entity speak.

Between Andrea's sobs, a low, garbled voice became audible. At first, we weren't sure if it was Andrea speaking to herself in another voice or if it was in fact a foreign sound. But Silvana nodded to me, verifying that there was a paranormal event in progress and that we should be on high alert. The distinction between Andrea's voice and the grumbling became clearer after about a minute of conversation. Andrea asked what it wanted and the voice responded with what sounded like "I, I, I, I, am, am, am, am . . . you, you, you, gonna, gonna, gonna, gonna, kill, kill, kill." Andrea interrupted and asked why it was making her feel bad and making her choke in front of her mommy and daddy.

That was about all Karen could take. The distraught mother broke free of her husband's arms and rushed to her daughter's side, screaming at the top of her lungs, "Get away from my daughter, you *thing*. Whatever you are! Stop that goddamn evil stuttering and say what you want from us!

You're not killing anyone here, you bastard!" Steven followed his wife to Andrea's side and hugged the girl along with Karen. During the confusion, I hadn't even noticed that Silvana had collapsed and hit the floor and was lying next to me semiconscious, apparently in a state of near exhaustion. I bent over to help her up, and she waved me off with a hand gesture. I looked around, stunned by what had just happened.

Andrea was sobbing, but was comforted by her parents who assured her that everything would be fine. The girl asked her parents if the man ran away and if he got to tell them what he wanted to say. Karen and Steven humored her as much as they could and said that they would all go away and never come back. It was all a bad dream, they said. But as it turned out, the eight-year-old girl knew better.

Later that day, we told Karen and Steve that we could not explain the night's events other than to say there had definitely been a paranormal event in the house. Silvana confirmed the presence and noted that it had left swiftly. But I warned them that that didn't mean the end of the problem. Unless we could uncover something more, I advised that they move from the Gray Lady.

We planned to stay another day in order to review the videotape and pick up the photos we had taken to the local photo shop for processing. The previous night's strange events unfortunately continued for us when we discovered that the videotape of Andrea's conversation was blank. There was no video or audio—just snow for most of the tape. As we walked to the photo shop, we turned over every possibility we could to try to figure out what had gone wrong with the video equipment. It had never failed us before, so we chalked it up to yet another unexplained element of the case.

At Jimmy's Photo, the proprietor, a native of the area, handed us our prints taken by the auto shutter camera. He asked, "Interested in the old Gray Lady, huh?" I was as discreet as possible and said we liked unique architecture, so as not to betray Karen and Steven's confidence. "Well, that house sure has its history," he said.

"How so?"

"Well, you know it was about Ol' Tom."

"Old Tom?" I asked.

"Yeah, the story was that Ol' Tom—who they used to call the town idiot 'cause he stuttered so much—went crazy and set his house afire on the very grounds where the Gray Lady stands today. They say that Tom's little girl choked and died from the smoke. 'Course, then there's them who say Ol' Tom couldn't warn his family about the fire 'cause of his stutterin' and all. Who knows about these crazy legends, huh, mister?" Jimmy said.

As we left the store, Silvana and I waited for who would be the first one to say it. I broke down and asked Silvana if she thought Tom's ghost was simply trying to tell someone—anyone—that he had tried to save his family? And the choking was his way of dramatizing what had actually happened? Silvana half-listened as she shuffled through the photos we just picked up from Jimmy. She stopped walking with one print in her hand and said, "Robert, look at this!" In the photo, which was aimed directly at Andrea's window, there was a streaking apparition exiting the area. The apparition had the "standard" wisplike appearance commonly associated with spirits captured on film. The time stamp correlated exactly with the time we had experienced the event in Andrea's room.

"It looks like the ghost took off," I said.

Epilogue

We showed Steven and Karen the incredible photo and hypothesized that perhaps Ol' Tom had finally gotten his message across and run off. We suggested that they tell everyone in town, in hopes that the spirit would be satisfied that he was finally exonerated and would leave them in peace. It was a hard sell, and if they had not experienced the event in Andrea's room themselves, they would have probably dismissed us as lunatics. But they were desperate and agreed to try it out for a week or two.

Two months later, the family called X-Investigations to tell us that everything was fine. Andrea was recovering well and there were no more disturbances. They did say, however, that they sometimes smell smoke, but that it's coming from the diner a few blocks away—they think.